DEANDRA DYCUS PRESENTS:

BEAUTIFUL

Resilience

BEST BOOK
AWARDS
FINALIST
AmericanBookFest.com

STORIES OF INSPIRATION ON LIVING THROUGH
A MOTHER'S GRIEF

CONTRIBUTING AUTHORS

THOMASENA COLBERT, VALERIA HORTON, JULVONNIA MCDOWELL,
WENDY MCINTOSH, STEPHANIE STONE, FALISHA CURLIN WALKER,
TISA WHACK, OLGA WILLIAMS, PAMELA WOODEN

Beautiful Resilience:
STORIES OF INSPIRATION ON LIVING THROUGH A
MOTHER'S GRIEF

ISBN-13: 978-1-7360431-0-3
Library of Congress Control Number: 2021908017

DEDICATION

Beautiful Resilience is dedicated to the young men and women that were taken from us too soon - our children. Although DeAndre is still here, he is not the same. All of my sons' hopes and dreams were taken from him the moment that bullet left it's chamber. I promised my son that I would forever be his voice. To my first born, I dedicate my fight to you as you have inspired me, through your own personal battle. Together we have become an inspiration for whoever would take a moment to listen. You are my hero.

To all of my family and friends who have been on this journey with me from February 1, 2014, this is for you! I could not and would not be in this place if you all had not loved me through it. I thank you with all of my heart!

Beautiful Resilience would not have come together without the nine beautiful women who made a decision to join me on this journey. To my survivor sisters, I salute and admire each and every one of you. I draw strength from your courage. I love you with all of my heart.

It is in loving memory, I dedicate this book to Monica, Christopher, Jajuan, William (a.k.a Mister), Dominique, Isaiah (a.k.a. Zay), Tyrell (a.k.a. Butta), Jayva, Rayshawn, and Paul.

TABLE OF CONTENTS

Photo credit: Eric Dycus

CHAPTER 1: Author - DeAndra Dycus

DeAndra Dycus is a native to Indianapolis, Indiana. She has her degree in Business Administration. She is a wife, mother of two and bonus mom of three, entrepreneur, dynamic speaker, transformation coach, author and national gun safety advocate.

DeAndra is most known for her gun violence advocacy work, stating that if her son can fight his way back to life, so can she. She has done just that! Ms. Dycus has spoken out against gun violence on several platforms including the Democratic Attorney General Association's National Conference with standouts such as Tish James of New York City. Mrs. Dycus's work has landed her in speaking engagements alongside Nancy Pelosi and the Honorable John Lewis. She was invited to the White House as a guest of President Obama, to take part in his plans to take executive action on gun safety. She has worked with Congresswoman Lucy McBath and spoken in press conferences with Senator Murphy and Representative Robin Kelly as well many other congressional leaders who are fighting for gun safety. In 2019 DeAndra, alongside *Moms Demand Action* Founder Shannon Watts, was a part of the first ever Everytown For Gun Safety Presidential Forum where she interviewed several democratic presidential candidates that included Pete Buttigieg. In 2020 DeAndra had the distinct honor of being the Democratic National Convention's Gun Violence Speaker. The courageous story of her strength and her son's survival have been seen on CNN and she has been interviewed by the likes of Brook Baldwin and Christi Paul. Their story has also been featured on BET.

DeAndre and DeAndra's story have been in several national publications including the New York Times, Washington Post, Huffington Post, People, Humanity, Vogue, Time, Ebony, and Essence. DeAndra is a Fellow for Everytown For Gun Safety and a City Gun Violence Lead. She is also a long-time member of Moms Demand Action for Gun Safety in America.

In 2015 DeAndra founded a non-profit organization called *Purpose 4 My Pain*. The mission of *Purpose 4 My Pain* is to be a resource and support hub to families who have been impacted by gun violence by providing support, mentorship, and advocacy training. The goal is to make sure that our loved ones are known for more than just another number.

This wife, mother, and entrepreneur has no plans on stopping. Her journey continues as she launches into coaching workshops, and an upcoming podcast. She continues to be a standout businesswoman. Her workshops include advocacy, self-care, and the power behind sharing your story. "My mission is to create a safe space and atmosphere for women who are in need of encouragement, healing, and support because God has given me a special dose of strength to assist and serve women in painful situations. I too have experienced sorrow, pain, and despair but have made it through by faith and resiliency. I want to share what I have learned throughout my journey."

CHAPTER 1: DIVINELY, DESIGNED, DESTINY

By

DeAndra Dycus

"Through my greatest pain, I have found purpose. When it hurts to the core, wait, be still, and watch God birth a masterpiece from it within you."
-DeAndra Dycus

The year 2000 was a momentous year for me in so many ways! I was graduating from high school, and the world was in a frenzy with all the talk of the world crashing at midnight. I remember being downtown with one of my best friends, we were seventeen years old, young, wild, and free. We began running down the street towards the Circle, in downtown Indianapolis, headed to watch the ball drop and just a little afraid of the Y2K taking place. Our hearts were pounding with anticipation of what was going to happen when that clock struck 12:00 am We stood, holding hands, more like squeezing hands in the arctic Indianapolis January chill when my nose began to bleed. Tiny droplets hit the ground and I began digging in my purse for some tissue to stop the bleeding, so my new tan-colored, figure-fitting dress, would not be ruined. Katie turned to me asking strangely, "Girl, why is your nose bleeding?" I had no idea. I said, "Maybe allergies." I was elated it stopped and did not hinder any of our New Year's plans. We were both seventeen, I was anticipating early high school graduation in the coming weeks and what the next chapter of my life would be away at college. I had no time for anything or anyone to slow me down.

Two days later I stood in the bathroom of my parents' home pulling my hair up for school, and there it was, again, more random droplets. At this point my curiosity was getting to me, so I began to surf the internet on reasons for random nose bleeds. Back then, we weren't using the term, "... Google it," we were still surfing the web. One of the first things that popped up was pregnancy. I gasped for a second, then thought, nope, that cannot be it. I had plans; I was college-bound. In high school I loved learning, I did not necessarily love school, but college life fascinated me. The parties, friends, but mostly obtaining a successful career. The Business Administration major is checked on all the college applications: Ball State, Central State, Indiana State, and the University of Kentucky. I was nervous yet excited about going out of state, I could not wait to get my acceptance letters.

Two weeks later, after consistent nosebleeds, unexpected vomiting, and nausea out of this world, I learned the search results of possible pregnancy could not have been more accurate. As I sat alone in the bathroom on the toilet seat, tears streamed down my face, as I stared at the two pink lines on the white stick. A wave of disappointment caused knots to form in my stomach. "How could I have been so ignorant and irresponsible", I spoke out loud, as if I were trying to convince myself of just how dumb I was.

I ran into my room and threw every college application into my pink and purple wastebasket. I laid in my white daybed wondering how in the world was I going to tell my mom that I was having a baby. I knew she would be home soon, so out of nowhere, I sat up and began writing her a letter. I knew I could not face my mother. I did not want to face the disappointment in her eyes. I rushed down the steps and threw the letter into the mailbox and mixed it in with that day's mail since the mail had just been delivered. I went back to my room and cried myself to sleep. "DeAndra", I heard her whisper, "wake up my love." My love? Oh, no, she did not notice the letter or thought it was junk mail and tossed it into the kitchen trash can, which was my initial thought. I can't tell her. "Yes ma'am", I whispered in a raspy tone. I had dried tear stains on my face and a box of tissue next to my pillow. "Wake up, I read your letter." I rolled over to face the window, I couldn't face my mom, she tapped my shoulder and told me it was okay to look at her. My mother went on to tell me that although she wasn't happy with my choices, she was glad that I was graduating from high school early, as she did, and that she would support me in keeping my child. She said not having it is not an option. I laid in my mother's lap and softly began to weep. I cried those tears because I was relieved, she did not count me out, but instead, she showed me at that moment what it means to love your child unconditionally.

Eight months later, on September 26, 2000, DeAndre DeWayne Knox, my first love, was born, after twelve hours of labor, at 3:12 p.m. I gave birth to an 8.7oz big, brown-eyed baby boy. I did not know what I was having, as my unborn child did not cooperate during the ultrasound. "Your baby is healthy," is all the technology would tell me, and that was enough for me. DeAndre was full of life! He was energetic and kept me going. Never in a million years did I think I would be a teen mother. Yes, this girl had goals and dreams, but DeAndre was a grounding force I did not know I needed until I had it.

Dre, as we affectionately called him, was intelligent and by the time he was headed to first grade his preschool and kindergarten teachers had labeled him gifted and talented and encouraged me to find a school that could handle his wit, charm, and natural ability to navigate every school subject. Ms. Knox, your son is going to be someone outstanding. We're not saying that as a cliche, but truly he has gifts on the inside of him. I thought wow, I was entrusted with such a special responsibility from God to nurture him and protect his gifts so that he could go out and be anything that he wanted to be. The responsibility felt heavy, but I was so proud to be his mom. The fact that we were 18 years apart did not hinder my ability to be a good mother, I embodied every essence of the title.

DeAndre and I became inseparable. When you saw me, you saw my son. When DeAndre was two years old, I married, and by the time Dre was four years old, he was a big brother. After five years of marriage, we divorced. It was not easy on my children, but the three of us became like three 'peas in a pod.' I genuinely enjoyed motherhood and all it brought me, even the late-night nosebleeds and tummy aches.

In his early years, Dre wanted to be a Marine Biologist. I hated swimming, but he and his younger brother had a love for water and animals. Darrius wanted to be a veterinarian. We began taking trips to different zoos across the Midwest and beyond to support their love for animals. Chicago's Zoo was one of our favorites. My kids' eyes lit up in the fascination of all the animals as soon as we stepped one foot past the entrance. Traveling was one of our passions. I was never afraid to plan a trip and pack a bag. I traveled a lot with my aunt growing up and I wanted my boys to have the same experience. I worked hard, not always making much money, but I knew how to stretch it to make things happen. Traveling at least twice a year was a must.

As Dre crossed over into middle school, he started to find himself, as most kids that age do, he was often called a class clown. Partly because he loved the attention and had a knack for telling jokes. Those jokes often lead to a teacher calling home.

He told me one day, "Mom, I think I'm a ladies' man." I said, "Son, excuse me?" We both laughed so hard that we began to choke. This sounded hilarious, coming from a twelve-year-old child, however by this time Dre was in the sixth grade, he was standing about 5'6, weighing 150 lbs., with glistening brown skin and big brown eyes. I knew the girls were watching him. His athletic build and wide bright smile made him easy on the eyes. Football was the highlight of his life, he often told me he was going to be rich and buy me a big house. He played football for six years while mixing in basketball and baseball as time allowed. He wasn't a natural, but he had heart. Dre remained consistent and even when he didn't get the playtime, he wanted you could spot him on the sidelines yelling with excitement for his friends. His grades remained consistent too. I always shared with him, "If football does not take you where you want to go, you have the brains that will."

I divorced my youngest son's father in 2009 and for many years, it was only my boys and me. The boys struggled with the divorce, but it created a time of bonding between the three of us. When the family saw us coming, we would always hear, here comes DeAndra and the boys. DeAndra, DeAndre, and Darrius. The thought of that bond ever being broken rarely crossed my mind.

*****

In December 2013, I stood at my kitchen sink and asked God what my purpose was. I was a 30-year-old divorcee with a decent job and two wonderful young men that called me mom. Life was good but I must admit I was yearning for more, a clear definition of me being "fearfully and wonderfully made".

On January 1, 2014, I hosted a New Year's Day brunch with some of my closest relatives and I presented a toast, thanking God for not allowing the rising gun violence in our city to come near our family. Celebrating the fact that my boys had positive male role models and from our family values and upbringing, that there was no real fear such tragedies would come our way. As a family we toasted, ate, and enjoyed our blessings.

That toast, that moment of gratitude, and the yearning for the purpose all came to a head on February 1, 2014, when a stray bullet shattered the window of the home my son had been dropped off at just a few hours prior. To receive that type of phone call is a parent's worst nightmare, your child's not coming home or not coming back to you the way you last saw them because tragedy struck.

*****

The un-ordinariness of February 1, 2014, should have prepared me for the explosive turn of events in my life. It was over fifty degrees outside and yet, the sun was shining like the powerful star that it is. I was feeling good, and if I may say so, I was looking good too. Everything about this Saturday afternoon was beautiful, but I had a weird feeling in the pit of my stomach. I attempted to ignore the nagging feeling but was quickly reminded of it when I looked out of the window of the Goodwill store I was shopping in and saw a young girl lying in the street, just steps from the sidewalk. It appeared an oncoming car had struck her. My heart instantly went out to the mother screaming for help near the entrance of the store. "Someone, help me!" The pain in her voice prompted me to grab my phone to check on my two boys. DeAndre and Darrius were at my best friend's house with her children while we did some Saturday morning shopping. Between the two of us, we had four boys, and they hated shopping. We were excited that two of the four were now teenagers and that they could watch their brothers while we escaped for some "girl time". DeAndre answered, but did not sound like himself. When asked what was wrong, DeAndre replied he had a headache. I thought maybe his brother was getting on his nerves. Dre, as we affectionately call him, rarely got sick with more than some occasional dizziness from long car rides. Darrius, the younger of the two, had recently been diagnosed with headache syndrome. From his laughter in the background, I could tell their roles were reversed at this moment. "DeAndre, take a Tylenol and lie down. Mom will be there shortly," I said. "By the way, I do not think you need to attend that birthday party tonight, there have been multiple shootings in our city and your mom is worried." My thoughts went back to the lifeless body, mere steps in front of me. Feeling helpless as it pertains to your child's health is such a heavy feeling, I was trying to avoid anything that would have me in that place. I prayed for that screaming mother, but I also thanked God it was not me. DeAndre went on to fight his battle, one he was not going to win with this scene playing out in front of me. "But mom," he whined. He was thirteen, tall and handsome, but would whine like an eight-year-old who has been repeatedly told "No". "DeAndre, we will discuss this when I get back, and that ends the discussion for now." I turned to my friend and began to explain to her why DeAndre would not attend. Her son had recently turned thirteen and wanted to celebrate his entrance into his teenage years with a group of other young men. DeAndre being his best friend could not imagine, not being there. The truth is I packed DeAndre a pair of clothes just in case I decided to let him go. A fresh white V-neck tee, dry and slim fit, was his style, a light purple colored pair of Levi's, and a white and purple pair of Jordan's that he had saved up money to purchase. I knew my son prided himself on being fresh.

That mother's intuition kicked in as I went to pick DeAndre and Darrius up later that evening. Another, "But mom," rang out in a whiny tone. This time I turned to my son and said in an unyielding voice. "Okay, you can go but I need the name of the chaperones and the full address of this party. Son, I also need for you to be on your best behavior, keep your hands to yourself, no touching girls. If you witness a fight, exit the home, and give me a call. If you get into a fight, I will allow them to take you to a juvenile, then I'll ride by waving to you daily until you are released," we both laughed. At that time, we lived near the juvenile center and I literally drove by on my way home daily for work. Although we shared a good laugh, DeAndre knew that I was not kidding. He said, "Mom, why do you have to always bring up jail time?" DeAndre was a good kid and him going to jail was the least of my worries, but so was the young man who was recently murdered in our city two weeks ago. Neither bullets nor unlawful perpetrators see the goodness in a kid, they only fire and disrupt lives. I explained to him that so often, that is the plight of the Black man when he is put in or puts himself in a situation that erupts in violence. The law rarely shows mercy to men of color. Yes, I had these conversations, often with my boys. I wanted their outcome to be different. I knew that would come with a price, but I was willing to pay it for them, for the two of them to be nothing less than outstanding men. "Okay mom, I love you and I promise not to touch any girls or get into any trouble". That was the last time my son ever spoke a word to me. I cherish that last conversation, like a young child who cherishes their favorite blanket, and they carry it everywhere they go. "I love you mom," is forever in my heart, those words go everywhere with me.

"So now faith, hope, and love abide, these three; but the greatest of these is love." 1 Corinthians 13:13

I was never truly worried about DeAndre's behavior at the party, it was everyone else's. My friend and her boyfriend dropped the kids off. They let me know that the neighborhood appeared safe and that when our group of children arrived the crowd would be manageable. My one request of them was neglected - they observed the neighborhood, saw a small crowd, and decided not to go in to meet the chaperones nor get a vibe of the home. The peacefulness of the outside had so little to do with the tragedy that was soon to come.

One-shot changed our lives forever. Twenty-two bullets riddled that home, with one drilling into the back of my beloved DeAndre's head. My son, my oldest, but still my baby, had been shot. He collapsed, a young girl applied pressure to his wound, and my friend's daughter sat beside him, with tears of confusion streaming down her face. I can only imagine the pain in her face and in her heart. This should have been her last worry.

A stray bullet was fired from an undisclosed type of gun from outside of the home. I was told DeAndre was dancing with friends at the birthday party, and I am almost positive that he had his eye on some pretty girl when a bullet pierced the back of his skull, not only shattering his skull but our lives. The effects were like a tornado ripping through a small town, no target, no true path, solely a creator of destruction, at least initially. Tornadoes often take lives and cause major damage, like a bullet, but they also bring about a spirit of humanity that is so rarely shown, the devastation of gun violence did just that for me.

Psalms 23:4: *"Yea, though I walk through the valley of the shadow of death, I will fear no evil: for thou art with me; thy rod and thy staff they comfort me."*

DeAndre "died" that night, but with the help of fast-acting EMT workers, they were able to intubate my son and perform CPR at the scene and life was back flowing through his body, barely, but it was there. My honor student, my athlete, my protector, and the first genuine "love of my life", was shot while he danced inside of the house by an unknown assailant who shattered my hopes and dreams for my son and the window that separated the assailant from my son. DeAndre was more frightened than a mouse being chased by a tomcat. I know at that moment he longed for his mother. It pains me to this day that I was not there to protect him or to take the bullet for him.

It took a reflection of faith and the feeling of love to awaken me. I hurt, but I knew if there was nothing else that I had to do, I had to live through it. My youngest son Darrius needed me, DeAndre, my wounded warrior was depending on me. It was in that darkness of hours I learned the meaning of being selfless. It was through my mother's selflessness that I learned to give of myself, but there is nothing that could truly have prepared my children and myself for the journey before us. The journey is divinely crafted for DeAndra, DeAndre, and Darrius. I often call it the Divinely, Designed, Destiny.

A whisper said, "it'll be okay!" and startled me amid my crying. Somehow it intensified the pain swirling around in the pit of my stomach, reminiscent of a woman in labor. I was hurting, being okay wasn't my reality at that moment. Have you ever experienced so much pain you struggled to grasp the concept of light or darkness? You simply feel like you are solely there, in a space all your own. That is the type of pain that had me paralyzed in that Emergency Room hallway. Why, is the word that plagued my mind. I was confused, I was hurt, and I felt like I was slipping away into the pain of a broken heart. It was seeking to consume me while stealing the me, I always prided myself in being. I had to stop and take a deep breath, I had to get a hold of myself. I had to reach back to my childhood and reflect on what had brought me this far in my life! At that moment I heard another whisper say, "Faith." It was then that my paralysis began to shift, when I opened my swollen and puffy eyes, I took a deep breath and looked around and every person that I loved, carried me through the toughest times and helped put a smile on my face, was there surrounding me. Another whisper pierced my conscience and reminded me, "You are loved." That reminder released an exhale from my soul that brought me peace, a peace that I still don't understand today but am forever grateful for.

"Now faith is the substance of things hoped for, evidence of things not seen." Hebrews 11:1

The next thirty-seven days, DeAndre fought for his life. Many mornings I woke up from a sleepless night, lying on a cot in the pediatric intensive care unit waiting room, grateful I was not awakened overnight by a nurse telling me to come and say goodbye. The doctors warned me daily that he was not going to survive, and I needed to decide whether to pull the plug. They kept speaking to his "quality of life, "if he were to survive at all. They warned me not to be selfish. They didn't have my faith, they didn't understand my prayers, and they didn't understand the prayers God was answering through Dre. They couldn't understand that by not giving a decision, I was standing in faith even though they could only observe him 0.1 from being brain-dead. As I looked at them through steely eyes, and I believe they witnessed what my voice couldn't convey, giving up is NOT an option. Seven days into our fight for survival, DeAndre opened his eyes. I knew my son was saying, "Momma, fight for me!" DeAndre's injuries, the absence of justice, the carelessness of the young man who shot my son, lax gun laws, and most of all, the promise I made my son, began my Purposeful Journey. The one I asked for but never conceived what came with it. I promised Dre if he would fight to live, I would be his ears, his voice, his arms, and his legs until God saw fit to restore his body to its intended state. Dre's shooting left a once tall, gifted, and talented thirteen-year-old young man non-verbal and paralyzed from the chest down. His diagnosis read "traumatic brain injury, non-verbal spastic quadriplegic". However, for me, I call him my miracle waiting to unfold.

"Purpose", there's that whisper again. This time I cried to God asking, "*How did we get here?*" He whispered directly into my Spirit, "*Remember you asked for purpose?*" In my heart, I wished with everything within me that I could have taken that conversation back. I did not want anything to do with this type of pain, no matter the purpose. "*Be careful what you ask for.*" I have heard that a million times in my life. I knew what was meant by it, but I am not sure if I ever thought much of it until the ask came to pass. We ask, but are we prepared for the answer? I think we have an idea but can never fathom the severity that brings our purpose into view. Oftentimes it catches us off guard, never realizing that everything we need is already within us.

In the aftermath of my son's shooting, I was desperate to find reasoning. I often asked, "Why us, Lord?" "*Why my baby?*" DeAndre had a promising future ahead. He was a young scholar. He was athletic and easy on the eyes. He was a caring big brother and a son that would lay down his life for his mother. Why is this a chapter in our story? So many people say you should not question God, but Jesus even asked for His cup to be taken from him as he was on the road to living out His purpose, the crucifixion. However, He followed His request with, *"Let thy will be done."* My asking "why" motivated my mindset and actions going forward. If this is our journey, then Lord let thy will be done. Show the purpose for our pain, God, and He did just that.

When Dre was released from the hospital and came home, I had no idea what awaited me. All I knew was that I wanted the opportunity to care for my son, as I had always done. The doctors tried repeatedly to discourage me from bringing Dre home, advising me that the care would be too great. DeAndre came home to us as a spastic quadriplegic who was non-vocal, with severe brain damage. I did not lose my son in the physical on February 1, 2014, but I mourned the loss of who he had the potential of becoming and who I had dreamt he would be.

I can see now, seven years later, what the doctors were trying to tell me. All I could grasp what that I needed to care for Dre as I had always done, it may have been better for DeAndre had he been placed in a residential care facility. The lack of education resulted in me making the best decision at the time, however, more education should be given to families who are abruptly faced with the full-time care of a loved one instead of insisting that they send them away. Machines, nurses, medication, and incontinence supplies now filled the family room of our home. The same family room that only six months before the shooting, Dre and his friends danced around celebrating his entrance into his teenage years.

A new chapter had begun in the days following Dre's arrival home, my heart consistently resided in a space of grief and gratitude. Gratitude, because my son beat every odd when he survived his catastrophic gunshot wound. Grief, because looking at him daily, bed-bound, and unable to communicate his basic needs, isn't who I imagined he'd be nor doing what I thought he'd be doing. This realization caused a type of heartache that I'm not sure that I'll ever intelligently put into words.

It hurts is all I could say in the early days following my new role as mom and nurse.

Loss is defined as the fact or process of losing something or someone. On February 1, 2014, I lost something and someone. I lost who DeAndre was and who he was to become. There is anguish in recognizing your child is in pain but not being able to relieve it. There have been many days while on this journey, I have experienced helplessness. I have witnessed Dre moaning in pain but is unable to put his feelings into words. During those times, I have witnessed a single tear rolling down my son's face. I sensed his eyes were screaming, "Help me, Mom." I felt myself take a deep and exhale it to hide my raging thoughts and wipe away my own tears. Then I remembered my commitment and rose to be everything my son needed, daily.

How I stepped up to the plate is the part of our journey that intrigues many people. I suppose I can understand why, but for me, I am only doing what I first promised my son and what, secondly, I feel any mother would do in the same situation. I have seen my son endure the pain I know my body could not withstand. In those moments when I have seen tears stream down his face but am unable to hear his voice articulate his needs, I question myself, my role, and if I am doing the right thing for him. Did I do the right thing? Was I being selfish in wanting my son to stay by any means necessary? The truth is the die was set on day seven. The day when Dre began breathing on his own, and those charged with his care slowly turned down the machines, and they were turned off; we watched the miracle, which is Dre, unfold before our eyes.

"So, Jesus said until him, "Unless you see signs and wonders you will not believe." John 4:48

I began thinking about my conversations with God and me questioning why He allowed this to be my journey. I recalled His word saying He would not put more on us than we can bear, and that thought led to me reflecting on His promise, never leave us nor forsake us.

Thirty-seven days after a stray bullet pierced my son's head and traumatized his brain, he was released into my care and the care of a supporting agency that would bring nurses in and out of our home. This was the beginning of the next chapter in our journey of fulfilling our individual and collective purpose. Oxygen tanks, monitors, tracheotomy supplies, hospital beds, and strangers in and out of my home. I often battled depression! The simplest things agitated and angered me. I rarely slept through the night as I had to do overnight medications and turn Dre to different positions to prevent skin breakdown. In those moments of uncertainty, I would often wonder how did we get to this place? The place where I am experiencing a version of Dre that I never imagined. A version who rarely showed emotion and when he did it was usually filled with great sadness while tears coursed down his face. I would give anything to know the thoughts that flowed through his mind. For four months, my son lived with a missing L-flap on the left side of his skull, resulting in his lack of emotions.

Dre's silence was deafening! Witnessing my son's pain, attending doctor's appointments three days a week, and dealing with all the challenges that come with someone surviving a gunshot wound pulled at my heartstring. I began thinking, "How does one do this alone?" "How do I change the narrative that every black male shot has a criminal history and comes from a broken and dysfunctional home?" All while realizing that through my pain I had to tell Dre's story.

Deciding to share our journey with the world changed my life. The call about advocating for my son and others like him, opened doors for me to meet courageous men and women who had been shot or who had lost someone close to them. The strength of these survivors astounded me. I was encouraged by their strength and unwillingness to give up, I was empowered and inspired to share my story with anyone and everyone who'd listen. This resulted in me getting involved with local groups who fought to end gun violence and who matched my passion for change. I never wanted another mother to feel my pain. DeAndre was still here but I felt like I had an open wound, something that kept festering. It hurt! The more painful it became to watch my son suffer, the more energized I became to advocate and be Dre's voice. Before I knew it, my prayer changed from me asking God "why" to me, asking God to show us what resilience looks like.

There were times when my pain was challenged. In the beginning, I was shocked at the lack of empathy that other people, who had suffered loss, had as it pertained to the loss we suffered. I spent many nights fighting with myself asking myself if I had a right to be a gun violence advocate because my son lived while so many had their kids when I didn't. Some even took their anger out on me and made awful comments due to the path I'd chosen to stand against gun violence. Their anger said I didn't have the right to be an advocate! I have to admit that hurt! But I learned early on, that we all have a different path to our grief journey. I realize "hurt people, hurt people," but I'd like to visualize a different outcome where "hurt people can help heal each other." It's all in how you apply your pain. I choose the latter. In my eyesight, there is no competition in pain, but above all else, I made Dre a promise, and their negativity was not going to keep me from upholding my promise. I began calling myself, "the mother who will never shut up nor shut up." I needed people to fully comprehend the reality of what surviving a gunshot wound looks like. I needed them to know that just because you survived didn't mean life went back to normal - in so few cases it rarely does.

AND IT BEGINS...

I was invited to New York City to train on how to share my story, it was an incredible experience. The connectivity and encouragement were powerful. Shortly after leaving New York City, I decided to start a nonprofit organization. I needed something to honor my son and to support others who have survived gun violence. Whether a victim, a survivor, and/or their family. The urge to support other women whose pain matched my daily struggle was overwhelming. That urge turned into action on Feb 1, 2015, Purpose 4 My Pain (PM4P) was founded, and we hosted our first "Pray 4 Dre Play 4 Dre," 5 on 5 Basketball Tournament. My family and I wanted to honor Dre's fight by celebrating what he loved, basketball. My son was shot less than 24 hours after playing his first and only seventh-grade basketball game. During that game, he scored 7 points. DeAndre's friends formed teams and played their hearts out for Dre. It was an astonishing show of community. The day was not solely about Dre, it was a space created to advocate and share the pain of gun violence that impacts many families, young men, and women. Mothers came from all over the city, wearing the faces of their children on t-shirts as their stand united against violence. It was a show of solidarity that I never imagined but spoke to my conversation with God when I asked Him to show me purpose, and He did just that.

The following year, in June 2016, we became a 501C3. P4MP has served over 500 families since its inception with 90% of its funding through private donors who support the work we are doing. It wasn't until 2020 that I sought funding through grants. My commitment to the vision and mission of the P4MP often resulted in the lessening of my bank account. I am thankful that I had the funds to do what my faith spoke to daily. I just wanted to do the work and support other women who were suffering on this journey. I felt myself becoming a connector. Connecting courage with strength, strength with hope, and faith with love and resiliency. I wanted people to know that their loved ones' lives and their voices mattered. I learned early in my grief journey that people who wanted to be heard and feel supported. They wanted to be heard telling anyone who'd listen that their loved one was more than just a number or 30-second news story.

Through P4MP's work, we started "A Woman's Pain" support group for women whose lives are impacted by gun violence. P4MP is also a resource hub for families in the immediate or late aftermath of gun violence. We provide resources as well as funding to assist with funeral services, groceries, utilities, and rent. We also create care packages for mothers in the immediate aftermath of the loss of their child. P4MP strives to be what I wanted and/or needed during our time of tremendous heartache.

Some days I feel my life is barely recognizable. As I continue to elevate our story and be the voice of my son, I now believe I am closer to answer the "why" I asked God to reveal on that dreadful night. God has opened more doors than I can count for people to hear of Dre's story and to learn about his continuous fight for survival. It's not easy penning these words but I believe they are necessary. His journey shows a different side to the public health crisis of gun violence - the injured victim. Gun violence injures over 200 individuals a day in the United States. The financial impact on communities can be viewed through Dre's survival and the financial obligation associated with his care that's well into the millions. The daily struggle of parents watching their child live after their experience with gun violence but losing control of their body, the ups, and the downs of the health of their child, and most of all, the waiting. The waiting is hard and heavy. The hardest part of the journey is waiting on a phone call, your loved one is sick and requires emergency care, all while waiting on God to perform a miracle, or anticipating the inevitable. It is the wait that causes me to cry when I'm alone in the midnight hour, but it is Dre's fight that encourages me to keep going. His fight has taken my faith to a place that profoundly moves mountains.

Our story has been seen and heard all over the world. We have been published nationally in Ebony, Essence, People Magazine, Vanity Fair, and most recently Time Magazine. I have had the distinct honor of visiting the White House, visiting with President Obama, and speaking with leaders from the United States Congress, including the honorable John Lewis and Lucy McBeth. I have been on many podcasts and radio shows and editorialized in the local newspapers and national magazines sharing Dre's story. Most recently, I was the gun violence speaker for the Democratic National Convention. It was simply incredible!

I am not boasting when I share our testimony of what it looks like to reside in a space of grief and gratitude. I have gratitude for the fact that as long Dre has breath in his body, that a miracle can be performed. I have gratitude for knowing my son's tenacity and strength are an inspiration to others. I welcome this space of gratitude because our story is not falling on deaf ears. Politicians are listening, and the youth are being encouraged to make positive life changes. Together, DeAndre and I are inspiring a generation. That inspiration gives me hope. I can honestly say, I never anticipated we would be in this place taking this journey. This journey has represented a place of pain, suffering, and uncertainty coupled with love, gratitude, and overwhelming appreciation. DeAndre, Darrius, and I are resting in a place of grace. That bullet did not get the victory in our lives even though we experience grief, daily. Grief, because I miss what was and what could have been in DeAndre. I have learned many things on this journey, but my greatest lesson is to cherish every moment! The Bible says in Matthew 6:34, "Therefore do not worry about tomorrow, for tomorrow will worry about itself. Each day has enough trouble of its own." I am motivated daily to focus on today, the love it brings, and the memories we create. I encourage everyone I meet to enjoy the moment. As much as we love something or a person they can be taken instantly and be replaced with immense pain! A pain that is often indescribable. Search out the purpose for the pain. As you begin your journey, watch God reveal pathways for you to navigate your new journey. I am certain He will be in your life, what He has been in mine, a very present help.

I found there is so much strength in giving back and sojourning with others who have trodden in familiar territory. Collectively you all can display what healing looks like as it leads to hope that encourages you to advocate, I called it Beautiful Resilience.

I Love My Son
By DeAndra Dycus

I love my son
When he wakes me in the middle of the night
When his cries began to cause me to ache
I love my son
When he yells Momma and I wanna change my name, thinking this boy is driving me insane
I love my son
When the teacher calls and I yell boy I'm gonna whip your tail… I'm so sick of your daddy going to jail!
I love my son
When the world doesn't understand your complexity... I promise I will always try to
When you want to retreat away when the interaction with society has simply been enough when the going gets tough. When enough is enough!
I love my son
When the world no longer understands your complexity of becoming a man. When I question the why's that led you to be set apart when societal thoughts clash with my heart…when my understanding gets clouded by visions of us being apart
I love my son

When I hold you at night, making you a motherly promise, that I can't be certain of, but I need you to be certain of, that everything will be alright…when I see the doubt in your eyes, when your flicker becomes a flame, and others are unsure how to tame

I love my son

When the pain causes you to yell out, and your big brown eyes gaze up at me when your voice is silent, but your heart speaks volumes

When I take my right thumb and wash the tears that only drop from one eye away, kiss your forehead, and you bashfully swipe that forever kiss off your cheek…when your spirit stays meek, but your expressions are yelling, let me speak!

I love my son

When you lie there and mumble, I understand confusion may at times give way to doubt, but still, believe God will bring us out

When the picture no longer fits the frame, and I realize it was all worth the pain

I still love my son

DeAndre Knox

JOURNAL PROMPT

Loss comes in all forms. It can be a job, a loved one, a relationship, or even the loss of material things.

I challenge you in this journal prompt to write a letter of release to your loss. Take a moment to get it out!!!! Share memories, pain, passion, and purpose. Joy truly comes in the morning when you get your release so that your personal mourning can come.

_____

_____

_____

_____

_____

_____

_____

_____

_____

_____

_____

_____

_____

_____

Photo Credit – Eric Dycus

CHAPTER 2: Author - Pamela Wooden

Pamela Brodie Wooden was born in Hopkinsville, Kentucky. She is a widow, mother of six, grandmother, and a great grandmother. She is an up-and-coming mental health advocate, who strives to end the stigma surrounding mental illness. Pamela is a Christian who is known for her positivity and uplifting others, for helping others in need, and providing resources to bring awareness to the challenges those in the mental health community experience.

Pamela is the founder of Christopher Goodlow Jr. Mental Health organization where they seek to bring the issues facing the mental health community to the forefront and stop the negative stigma they experience. She has put together several programs for those suffering from a mental illness and for the families of those who care for a loved one with a mental illness. She has invited mental health professionals and the crisis intervention officer to educate others on how to deal with individuals having mental health crises and/or manic episodes. She is also working with other organizations to help engage in programming, to stop gun violence, and serve as an mental health advocate.

CHAPTER 2: DYING TO LIVE AGAIN

By

Pamela Wooden

I have faith that my life's journey will continue forward because God is guiding my way. James 1:1-6

In 2015, my world changed forever; it was one of the most devastating years for me and my family. After months of watching my husband fight, he lost his battle to cancer and passed away in March. It was tough for me to pick up and keep going without my life partner. After eight long months of struggling to adapt to a new normal without my husband, I faced yet another tragedy.

On December 12th of the same year, Indianapolis Metro Police Department officers murdered my son. When I received the call, I felt like I was on a never-ending roller coaster. That day was a day from hell. My son, Christopher Goodlow, Jr., suffered from Schizophrenia with Bipolar Disorder. He was experiencing a manic episode and was standing outside with only his socks and boxers on. Neighbors witnessed him outside with a pocketknife and cuts on his body. The police were called, and dispatch was told a male appeared to be suicidal. The officers arrived at the scene, without crisis intervention, a mental health specialist, or Chaplin in attendance. The unprepared and ill-equipped officers immediately jumped out of their patrol cars, pointing their guns while shouting for my son to drop the knife. Mind you, he's Schizophrenic with Bipolar tendencies and was having a manic moment.

My son did not put the pocketknife down but started to jump around. The officers shot him four times. To make matters worse, IMPD did not bother to notify me they'd murdered my son. A neighbor grabbed my son's phone during the aftermath of this tragic event and called me. All he said was, "*Someone has killed your son.*" Before I got to the scene it was already blasted all over social media. A different neighbor had aired it live on Facebook and captured my son being murdered.

I called my daughter and told her about the call, I received, informing me my son had been murdered. All I knew was I needed to get to him right away. As I arrived at my son's apartment, I could see the police tape and neighbors milling around talking. As I got closer, I could see my daughter's despair. They had already taken my son's body and cleaned the blood up off the ground where his body laid. The officers involved in the shooting were not on the scene when we arrived, but the officers there were dismissive to both me and my family.

This was a day from hell! I was lost, I was hurt, I was angry, and I was heartbroken. I told myself that if I had gone to his apartment before going to the store, my son would still be here. I could not eat; I could not sleep and all I thought about was how my son was shot down by individuals who had promised to protect and serve us. How was I going to explain this to Christopher's two beautiful daughters? Especially since it took me two weeks to grasp the finality of what happened, and to decide to bury my son.

As time went on, I was faced with the harsh reality that IMPD and my son's mental health providers failed him. I found out that his mental health counselor was not doing regular wellness visits as expected, and the doctor changed his medication from a monthly injection to pills. The doctors nor the counselor notified me of any changes to his care.

Once I had the strength to go into his apartment, we found pills he was hiding, which led me to believe whenever the counselor did come, they didn't watch him take his medication.

I started to ask God for understanding, "*Why did my son have to be killed like that?*" I continued to blame myself and asked God for forgiveness for whatever I did to cause this to happen. During my conversations with God, one scripture stood out to me, Proverbs 3:5, "*Trust in the Lord with all your heart and lean not on your own understanding.*" I finally said, "*Okay Lord, I trust you.*"

In March 2016, a close friend of the family visited, and during the visit, he said to me, "*It's time for you to bring awareness to mental health.*" At that moment I decided to stand up for what I believed in and recognized the opportunity for me to be a voice for those who suffer from mental illness. The Christopher Goodlow, Jr. Mental Health Organization was birthed during that life-changing conversation. While I was creating the organization, the IMPD had put together a crisis intervention team (CIT). My family and I started putting on programs to bring awareness and resources to the area that people were unaware of. I would invite the CIT officers and other mental health professionals to come out and speak, to provide education to families dealing with loved ones who may have a mental illness and to those suffering from a mental illness.

Around the same time, I created my organization, I also joined a women's organization, an immensely powerful and supportive group of women. In this group, we talked about the tragic events we experienced, as we learned how to lean on one another for encouragement, inspiration, and support to uplift our spirits. I was learning how to be less angry and more vocal. As I ran the organization and worked with our clients, I realized I was being healed while helping others.

Just when I thought things could not get any worse, in 2018 my mother became ill. We couldn't figure out what was going on with her. On July 16, 2018, my second oldest daughter, Monica Pirtle, was murdered in a car outside her home. It was literally two and a half years after losing my son! At around 12:30 a.m., my son-in-law came into my room and said, *"Come on, we have to go!"* I asked what's wrong and with tears in his eyes he said, *"Someone killed Monica!"* I said, *"Monica, who, not my Monica?"* He said, *"Yes, Ms. Pam, let's go!"* At that moment, everything went black! I was in disbelief, not another child, not my daughter, one day before her birthday. All I could say was, *"Lord, not another child!"* This could not be true!

I got up and got myself together as much as I could and went to my daughter's house. As we arrived, I saw that yellow crime scene tape again. This time, there was a homicide van and the Chaplin. I instantly felt like I was about to pass out. I looked up to God and continued to say, *"Lord, not again. Not another child!"* I was sitting in the car, my nephew came and got me out of the car and took me into my daughter's house. I continued saying to God, *"Not another child." "Lord why?"* The detective approached me and started to explain to me what had happened and what they had gathered so far. Monica's three daughters were in the house when it all occurred and heard the gunshots. They did not know it was their mother until the detective came to the door. Again, I looked to God and said, *"Not another child!"*

I felt like I was in the twilight zone and could not find my way out. My daughter had gone to the movies with her youngest daughter's father and never returned home. I started to think about the conversation we had on Sunday, July 15, 2018, when she said it was time for me to live my life and how pretty I am, how pretty my smile is, and was encouraging me. She was telling me about all her business plans. Monica was highly creative and an artist. To date, the case is not resolved, and we are still hoping for justice for Monica.

As I sit and think about my children, I sometimes smile, and other times, I cry. Monica and Christopher were my two goofiest children. Even though Christopher had a mental illness, he tried hard not to let that keep him down. He smiled all the time and loved his family. Monica was a painter and she decorated homes. She had a passion for fashion in all sorts of ways. Now I have five granddaughters who have a parent killed due to gun violence.

I have guardianship over Monica's youngest daughter. She reminds me of her mother daily. She continuously asks about her mother and if she will ever come down from heaven to visit her. The hardest part for me is trying to explain to a four-year-old how death works. Anger would rise up in me sometimes while trying to explain it to my granddaughter because it had taken its toll on me emotionally.

On Thursday, July 19, 2018, we took my mother to get a biopsy and was informed by the doctor she had Stage 4 cancer. I looked up and said, "*God, have we not been through enough?*" Then I left the room to cry. I did not want my siblings or my mother to see me cry. I looked up to God again and said, "*God, I thought you said you will never leave me or forsake me?*" Still, no answer from God. I had to admit, my depression was at an all-time high resulting in me not sleeping for over seventy-two hours. I decided to get some help and scheduled an appointment with my doctor and a counselor. The doctor and counselor both were in shock and asked me, "How are you still standing?" All I could say was. "*Nobody, but God!*"

As months went by my mother's cancer progressively got worse, her treatments weren't working, and she did not have enough strength to go through any aggressive treatments. My siblings and I made the tough decision to put her in hospice at her home. The doctor gave her six months. She outlived those six months but passed away on September 1, 2019, the day after her birthday.

Outside of my children, my mother was my whole life. I couldn't ever imagine as a child watching my mother grieve the losses of five out of ten of her children and her husband, would be one of my greatest life lessons. It was the glow on her, as well as the heartache that I witnessed from her, that aided and guided me as I dealt with the biggest heartaches of my life: the loss of my two children and my husband. Who would have ever imagined my mother and I would experience the same type of loss? When you birth children, you never imagine their beautiful souls would leave this earth before you. Losing my children was a heartbreaking loss for my mother too. My Mom, along with her righteous prayers, carried me and my remaining children through what has been an unimaginable journey.

Now, my mother is gone, however, her beautiful spirit and the seed of faith she planted in my life lives on forever. I often cry out to the Lord saying, "*I cannot do this by myself.*" I am exhausted, weary, and overwhelmed by all that's expected of me. It seems as if everyone wants a piece of me and I have nothing left to give. I am trying to please everyone, encourage and support everyone, love everyone, and I have poured out everything I have. If I am being honest, I feel empty, frustrated, and alone!

As I think about my mother, I remember one of her favorite scriptures, she'd tell me to read it and then pray. Matthew 11:28 says, "*Come to me all you who are weary and burdened and I will give you rest.*" If you think about everything, I have been through in the past five years or longer, I'd say it's about time for some good news. Regardless of what's happening around me or the news reports of the violence, crime, and tragedies that happen daily, my faith tells me that God is with me! Even during those times when God seems so far away, I still believe God is with me.

Although God's word says He will not put more on us than we can bare, my family experienced loss after loss due to the corona pandemic.

Three aunties and a cousin passed away in May and their memorial services/funerals were held in May 2021. I asked God, *"…how much more, LORD? We are still grieving from the loss of my mother."* I remember, one day when I cried while sitting in my car, and during my emotional breakdown, I heard a voice that sounded like my mother's voice, telling me *"God will restore your soul."* Once the words were spoken, my tears dried up and I began praying Psalms 23:3, *"He restores my soul; He leads me in the paths of righteousness for His name's sake,"* while asking God to make me whole: emotionally, mentally, and physically. A few days later, I was talking with God, and I was inspired to begin to live again and continue my journey to living God's purpose for my life.

There are so many things I want to do going forward. I plan to continue operating the Christopher Goodlow, Jr. Mental Health Organization to provide resources to those diagnosed with a mental illness and their family/loved ones to ensure they receive the treatment/care they need. I will also fight to end the stigma surrounding those suffering from a mental illness because my family and I do not want to see another person while experiencing a mental health crisis, lose their life like my son, Christopher, did. By pursuing God's purpose, I have truly found my RESILIENCE…

In Loving Memory:
Monica Pirtle and Christopher Goodlow, Jr.

JOURNAL PROMPT

God has truly kept me and continues to strengthen me so that I will not give up. It has been a trying and hard time for me especially after losing my two children. I thank God for His grace and mercy, keeping me in good health and strength to raise my four-year old granddaughter. Have you ever felt like giving up or dying to live again?

_____

_____

_____

_____

_____

_____

_____

_____

_____

_____

_____

_____

_____

_____

_____

_____

_____

_____

_____

Photo Credit - Sarah Matteson Photography

CHAPTER 3: Author - Stephanie Stone

Stephanie Stone was born and raised in Macon, Georgia. She was the youngest of three and the only girl. Stephanie moved to Atlanta, Georgia in 1991 and worked for C & S Bank for several years. On May 4, 1998, Stephanie delivered a beautiful son who she named, Paul Reginal Sampleton Jr. In 2007, Stephanie obtained her Bachelor's degree in Management from Shorter College. Stephanie's career path had changed to healthcare as she began working with Gentiva Healthcare. On December 19, 2012, Stephanie's only child, Paul's, life would be taken by gun violence.

After Paul's tragic death, Stephanie became Paul's advocate, his voice, the voice for so many other survivors and victims of gun violence. She joined *Moms Demand Action for Gun Sense in America* as a volunteer. The bullets that took her beloved son's life, ignited a new beginning for her own life. Stephanie was put on an unexpected journey of advocacy, fighting bad gun laws, meeting with legislators, and helping and mentoring survivors.

Stephanie fights tirelessly with survivors as a Program Manager with *Everytown for Gun Safety*. She's spoken on platforms in New York with Julianne Moore, Congresswoman Lucy McBath, Shannon Watts and several survivors about the impact of gun violence. Stephanie has also appeared in several news outlets and national magazines as she's shared her story about Paul and gun violence prevention. Stephanie's faith, family and friends have kept her grounded and hopeful during the darkest aspect of her life. Stephanie loves God and she knows her story is a testimony to help others. She lives by the motto of: "It's not about how long you live, but how you live." Although, her Paul only lived fourteen years, she continues to share his memory often. Paul made a great impact on those who knew him, and Stephanie is so honored to keep his legacy alive.

CHAPTER 3: FINDING PURPOSE AND JOY IN THE MIDST OF PAIN

By

Stephanie Stone

"When we lose someone we love, we must learn not to live without them, but to live with the love they left behind".

- Anonymous

I remember being five years old and having playtime tea in my room with my dolls. As I was serving imaginary tea to my favorite baby doll, I found myself having a strange conversation with her. I distinctly remember saying to my doll, *"Daddy will die first, then Momma, then Tracy, then Kenny, and then me."* I am not sure why death was on my young and innocent mind, but for some reason, I was curious. My dad was listening from the other room as I played. Hearing my conversation, he came in and sat down to talk. He began by saying, *"Steph, I heard you talking about death."* Then I remember him asking, *"Why are you thinking about death?"* He delicately informed me that death did not work the way that I was explaining to my doll. Death does not take people in age order. Anyone can die at any time. I remember him saying, *"We will all die one day,"* and then encouraging me to live, have fun and not worry about dying. Although I was frightened hearing my dad's words, I also felt safe because he was my protector.

Twenty-nine years later, I would speak to my son, Paul, at the same age, about death. Paul came to me and asked me about God and wanted to know where God lived. I recalled the childhood conversation I had with my dad about God. I remember telling Paul God lived in the sky, in a place called Heaven. Being curious, Paul continued with a barrage of questions like, "How do you get to Heaven? Who can go?" and so forth. I sat down with Paul to try to respond to his unanswerable questions as gently as possible. I told him that one day we would all get a chance to meet God in Heaven, but not for a long time. He had to continue to be a good boy, listen to his parents, do well in school and simply be a compassionate person. He then asked, "*What does it mean to die?*" I told him, what my father had shared with me, that one day everyone dies, but he did not have to worry about dying just be a kid and have fun. A few years later, death became more real to him.

In February 2009, I was taking Paul to Princeton Elementary in Lithonia where he was a fifth grader. Traffic was backed up and I knew I was going to be late for work. Forty-five minutes later, I dropped Paul off in front of the school, turned out of the parking lot, and headed to work. Later that day, I would find out that the traffic was backed up due to a second grader being hit by a car in front of the school, and he'd succumbed to his injuries. I remember feeling heartbroken. When I picked Paul up, he asked if I had heard about the little boy. I told him that I had. Paul stared out the window and I began some small talk to break the silence. Paul looked at me with sadness and simply asked, "*Is that little boy going to meet God?*" I told him, "*Yes, he was.*" He then proceeded to ask, "*Is God a mean person?*" I told him that God isn't mean, but I understood his little mind was trying to make sense of the boy's death. I had to be truthful with my son about life and its unexpected events. I told Paul, "*God wanted this little boy to meet Him, and although his parents would be sad, they would always have his memories and when the time came, they would see him again.*" He asked, "*What if something happens to you, Mom?*" I told him that he would have his dad and sister, and he would be fine. And besides, I was not dying that day. He smiled at me, reassured.

During the summer of 2012, Paul and I relocated to Grayson, Georgia. We moved into a red brick, three-bedroom townhouse in a quiet neighborhood. Paul was a fourteen-year-old teenager who would be starting his freshman year at a new school. Although he was a little nervous starting a new school as a freshman, he was excited to play football with the Grayson Rams. Grayson's football team was exceptionally good, and Paul was anticipating a starting spot. Paul was confident he would be a starting player on the freshman team, but he had some butterflies being the new kid on the block.

On Paul's first day of school, he got up extra early. He decided to wear some camouflage pants, a blue and orange Met's jersey and matched his outfit with some blue and orange Nike sneakers. He was in an excellent mood, and I was excited for him. Paul quickly made friends with some players on the football team, and he made friends with some girls, as I knew he would. Paul was a 'people person,' he instinctively knew how to manage these types of situations. I remember when Paul was in the fifth grade there was a classmate who was being picked on and was struggling to make new friends. Paul was right there to help relieve the anxieties for this kid being the new student in the class. Paul's teacher told me, *"that kid needed Paul to lift his spirits."*

As Paul got acclimated to his new school, I was 'on him,' making sure he kept up with his studies. Initially, Paul did have some struggles balancing school and football, but he was making steady progress. He knew good grades would be the only way he could continue sports. *"School first!"* I always said. As the first semester was coming to an end and the Christmas holidays were about to begin, Paul started studying for his finals. He needed to focus on his algebra, and he worked extra hard with his tutor.

Wednesday morning started off as a typical day. It was the last day of school before Christmas break, and he had finals. I got Paul up around 5:30 a.m. to start getting ready for school, as I prepared for work. I had to yell a few times before Paul got moving, but he eventually started making some progress. Paul was excited - it was the last day of school before a long winter break. As the morning progressed, I went into the kitchen to prepare one of Paul's favorite meals, a breakfast of eggs and waffles. As usual, we were running late, and Paul came downstairs to the kitchen wearing blue True Religion shorts and a white t-shirt to match. I remember saying *"Paul, it's cold outside, you need a jacket!"* He grabbed a black Nike jacket and his red "Beats" headset as we headed to the garage. As I drove Paul to school, we drove in silence while he ate his breakfast. I started the conversation by reminding him to take his time on his finals and to concentrate. I recall him replying, *"I will Mom."*

As I pulled up to Paul's school to let him out of the car, I told him that I loved him and to have an excellent day. Paul turned to me and said, *"Mom, give me a dollar?"* I handed Paul a dollar, he got out of the car and started walking towards the school. I glanced in the back and noticed he left his jacket on the seat. I started to yell after him to come back to the car, but the parking lot was congested, and I was being motioned to keep moving. I remember thinking, *"He'll be fine, it'll warm up later."* It was 6:50 a.m. and this would be the last time I would see my son, my only child, alive.

Paul's dad and I went our separate ways when Paul was four years old. Although we were no longer together, we maintained an excellent relationship. Paul's dad would often pick him up from school. However, on December 19, 2012, he planned to pick him up from our home and take him to his trainer for baseball practice. Paul wanted to sharpen his baseball skills because tryouts were going to start after Christmas break. Grayson had an early release on this day and Paul knew to go straight home and to call me once he was inside the house.

I was at work and I glimpsed at the time, realizing I had not yet heard from Paul. It was around 11:45 a.m., Paul should have been home by then. I called the house several times and there was no answer. I called Paul's dad, and he hadn't heard from Paul either. He reassured me that he was heading to the house to pick Paul up for practice, and he would call me once he arrived. I was feeling uneasy. It was not like Paul not to answer the phone, and he knew he could not go anywhere without permission. Paul's dad called me once he arrived at the house, and he said, *"Paul isn't answering the door."* I immediately got upset, thinking, *"Where is he?"* His dad decided to drive around to the school to make sure Paul had not missed the school bus, but he was not there.

It was six days before Christmas and four days before my forty-fourth birthday when I found myself racing home from work in Sandy Springs to Grayson in gridlock traffic on 285 East. I did not realize my Silver Honda Accord could go so fast as I darted in and out of traffic. Paul's dad had called me back and only told me to get home as fast as I possibly could. I remember my mind was racing, not knowing what to expect. I even picked up my cell phone and called 911 to see if I could get some information. I was told someone would call me back. I remember screaming in my car as my tears were flowing. I knew it was something horrible, but I did not want to imagine what. My heart was filled with so much anguish, but I kept driving as fast as I could to see what was going on with my only child.

As I entered my sub-division, I noticed the yellow tape blocking the entrance to my street. Paul's dad met me at the entry point and looked me in my eyes. I remember his lips moving, but I was in a state of shock. He told me Paul was dead. I looked at him, and he said it again, only this time, he added, *"Someone shot Paul."* Even now, I am not able to clearly remember what happened next. I just remember being numb. It was like a dream. I asked if I could see my son and the police would not let me. I called my mom, my aunt, and some family members, and from that point, things became a blur. When Paul's dad went back to our home after checking for Paul at the school, he decided to check the garage. He then entered our home through the garage only to find our son shot to death in the kitchen where I had cooked him waffles and eggs that morning.

Paul Reginal Sampleton Jr., an 8 lbs. 2 oz, baby boy, was born May 4, 1998, and had grown into a precocious, athletic, intelligent, fun-loving kid with the biggest smile that lit up any room he was in, was the target, of a planned home invasion. I later learned that some kids at Paul's school plotted to rob him of his sneakers by beating him up. One of the kids in the plot was a freshman player on Paul's football team, who I had given rides home several times after practice. There were two other teens involved in this plot. One of the teen's uncles and his older friend decided that if Paul had nice clothes and shoes this would mean we had other items of value in our home. Paul, like most teens, owned nice shoes and clothes. Paul developed a special love for sneakers, and he had built quite a collection. I would not have ever imagined my son's life being taken from him over some material items. A kid who had so much love to give, who had a heart of kindness and who wanted so much out of life, was gone, taken in an instant by greed, evil minds, and a gun. We were devastated!

The day of Paul's funeral, I felt as though I would not make it through the service. My breathing was rapid, my heart was shattered, and I remember yelling, *"This is not fair!"* Later that evening Pastor Johnson, who gave Paul's eulogy, called me. He told me, *"It isn't fair for Paul's life to have been stolen. And it is okay if you are angry with God, but you can't stay angry."* And I was definitely angry! I wanted to know why He allowed this to happen to a kid who had so much life and love to give. I did not have any answers, but I had prayer. *"Weeping may tarry for the night, but joy comes with the morning."* (Psalm 30:5) I wondered when my tears would stop, and would I ever have joy again?

Paul is the first thing I think about in the morning and the last thing I think about at night. I relive our weekly dinners at his favorite restaurants. We would go out to dinner every Thursday to catch up, bond, and decompress from the week. Paul loved going to Longhorn Steakhouse, Chili's, or for Japanese hibachi - his absolute favorite. I miss dropping him off at school and receiving a text message from him around 9:00 am asking me to bring him Chick-fil-a. On Sunday mornings, I would make pancakes for breakfast, and we would sit and eat together at our dining room table. After his passing, I stopped cooking pancakes and even stopped sitting at the table. It felt weird to dine alone.

During the summer, Paul and I would often travel. He loved staying in hotels and exploring different places. I wanted to give Paul the things my family could not afford when I was a child. When I was younger, my family did not travel, and when we did, it was to my grandparents' home in Kentucky. I wanted Paul to see the world and experience new things, sights, and people. I remember our first trip to Disney World. It was my first trip, too, and I was just as excited as he was. We had so much fun – most of all I remember our joy and laughter. I often imagine what Paul would be doing now as a young man. This is all I have left - my memories and imagination. I still cry, but I've decided to keep moving each day.

Over time and from those bullets, emerged a new Stephanie. I have become an 'accidental activist'. I became a counselor and a comforter to other survivors in my new truth. I never envisioned this would be my life, nor did I imagine my life without Paul. I did not ask for a lifetime membership in this awful club, yet here I am. December 19, 2012, was the beginning of something I could not have ever dreamt of. I became Paul's advocate, his voice, and the voice for so many other victims and survivors of gun violence. Paul's death was the catalyst that ignited something unexpected but necessary in me. It ignited a passion, determination, and empathy to help others who have experienced the trauma and pain of gun violence in me. I started connecting with so many families who were in pain due to the gun violence that touched their homes and ripped apart their families. It reminded me that I would always be Paul's mother. On average, over one hundred people die each day from gun violence and hundreds more are wounded. The violence is heartbreaking! When will it end?

A year before Paul's death, a local thirteen-year-old boy was found dead. He had been stabbed multiple times and then shot. The death of this young man upset Paul and his friends. One of his friends attended school with the young man, so it hit them hard. Paul was bothered about this to the point that I would wake up and find he was sleeping next to me in my bed. I tried to comfort and reassure him it would be alright, and he had nothing to fear.

My heart aches so much when I think about what my son endured on his last day of life. His dad and I tried to protect him from the things that would hurt or destroy him. Yet when he needed us the most, we weren't there for him. I struggled with 'survivor's guilt' for a long time. I found myself experiencing something I had not heard of until Paul's death. I can't tell you how many times I negotiated with God, being assured God is not "mean", and begging God to send Paul back to me. Being angry was an understatement, I was indignant. How do I go on with life without my son? So many thoughts passed through my mind, as I grieved the death of my son. I was alone and scared.

In February 2013, I received a call from Gwinnett County law enforcement informing me they had made an arrest in Paul's case. I was relieved, but also anxious. Who killed my son and why? They initially arrested three teenagers from Grayson, one of whom pretended to be friends with Paul. I was stunned. A few weeks after the arrest was made, I was asked to do an interview at one of the local news stations. I remember driving to Atlanta with my aunt feeling so much angst. I arrived at the news station and the reporter placed a microphone on my collar as he prepared me for the interview. He started the interview by asking me how I was doing. He then proceeded to ask me about the arrests made in my son's murder. All of a sudden, rage burned within me. I started calling Paul's killers "cockroaches." I was so full of anger; I could not think straight. The reporter looked at me and simply said, "Tell me about Paul." My heart melted! It was like my mind and my body instantly metamorphosed into another person, Paul's mom. I was delighted to share stories about my beloved son. I talked about how smart Paul was and how he loved his family and friends. I spoke about Paul being an athlete who wanted to attend Florida State and major in Marine Biology, even though he could not swim a lick. I shared with the world a story about a person they would never get to know or love. I knew, then, that it was my duty to keep Paul's memory alive. The fire of purpose was ignited, and I began the journey to determine what I needed to do to honor Paul, help me grieve, and to help others who have experienced what I experienced. The reporter turned what would have been a disastrous interview into something meaningful; and a new beginning for me. I never imagined recognizing my purpose and beginning a new life's journey after burying my son, my only child.

My aunt and I drove back to Macon after the interview. She teased me about the interview and how I called Paul's killers "cockroaches." I realized then I could not share Paul with the world if I let anger consume my heart. I had to learn how to channel my anger into action. I did not want Paul to be forgotten and I knew people would only remember the anger and not my son if I continued on this path of rage. I needed to fully connect with my purpose.

In November, prior to Paul's death, Jordan Davis was murdered. I remember during a conversation with Paul we discussed the senselessness of the murder and the reason for the murder: loud music. It wasn't until January 2013 when I decided to send a Facebook message to his mother, Lucy McBath. I had been following Jordan's page on Facebook. Within moments, Lucy's attorney reached out to me. He assured me that he would have Lucy call me. She called me the next day. We talked for over three hours and it was as if we had known each other for years. We were instantly connected. The tragedy we both suffered brought us together. It was destiny. Lucy was volunteering with Moms Demand Action for Gun Sense in America, and she was just getting fired up. She invited me to join in with the Georgia Moms to work on Georgia's wicked gun laws, and I did just that. I experienced an unexpected comfort - it felt right. I found my purpose! It was to save lives! I knew I would not stop until we had safer gun laws in Georgia and our country. I turned the worst pain anyone could ever imagine into action. I wanted the world to know Paul lived, his life had meaning, and his death was not in vain.

Over time, I understood grieving was not a linear process and I had to find joy in life, somehow. In 2014, during the anniversary of Paul's death, I decided to do something different to honor Paul. I did not want to keep going to his grave with family and friends yearly to release balloons and cry. It was like having a funeral for Paul all over again, and it was taking a toll on me as well as my mom and dad. I decided to invite Paul's friends for wings, laughs, and conversation - I wanted a place for Paul's friends to remember my son in a special way. I lived with the ugliness of his death daily, and I wanted a space to share in the joy of someone who was not only important to me, but so many others.

During the first outing, it was overwhelming because his friends were juniors in high school heading towards their senior year. I recall telling them that I knew as the years went by, fewer of them would be attending and that I understood - life goes on. I told them, *"But one thing I know for sure, you all will always carry Paul wherever you go in life. He is forever in your hearts."* The remarkable thing was I was wrong. As years have gone by, more of his friends have attended the anniversary outing. They call me a few weeks before the anniversary date to confirm we are still meeting. This makes my heart smile to know Paul is still being thought of by his friends who are now out of college and starting their adult lives. These kids needed me as much as I needed them. Through each of them, I see Paul and that brings me so much comfort.

The people who killed my son are now in prison for the rest of their lives. We went to court in September 2014, and it was grueling. For a long time, I wrestled with *"Why? Why Paul?"* I came to accept that I would never get an answer. I am relieved they will never get another chance to hurt another person or family. I sometimes think about forgiveness and what that would look like; however, I do not let the people who killed my son consume me. I have an awesome circle of family and friends who keep my spirits lifted. It brings great joy and meaning to my life, helping other survivors through my work with Everytown For Gun Safety as a Survivor Program Manager.

Grief is a day-by-day process and I have learned it is okay to have bad days. It is expected. As survivors, we learn to live with the giant elephant in the room. Grief takes time. Occasionally, the elephant decides to stomp on my toe, it's painful, and I let the tears flow. I allow myself to feel, to hurt, to scream, and to reflect. I love looking at and sharing pictures of Paul. I am so glad he was not the typical child who avoided cameras. My Paul loved taking pictures. For me, pictures are a portal to your existence - a reflection of your life. Pictures prove you lived and show how you did it. Although brief, my Paul certainly lived a full life.

I know my son is proud of me and my new perspective on life. God trusts me enough to do the work I am doing to help others and I will not let Him down! I would never let Paul down, either. I thank God for choosing me to be Paul's mother and I don't take it for granted. In my son's brief time on earth, he touched many lives and forever changed many hearts. One thing I have learned on this unexpected journey is it is not about how long you live; it is about how well you live in the time you have. What legacy will you leave behind once you are no longer here? Who would expect something so tragic could be turned into a life's mission? Paul only lived fourteen years, but his legacy remains, and his memory lives on in my family. I even have two nephews who are named in his honor. Paul's friends continue to honor and remember him, too. Most of all, his light shines through me, his dad, through my work, and through my joy. I have been able to travel and explore the world. Although Paul is not with me physically, I know his spirit is. I am now able to make pancakes and sit at my kitchen table, something I had completely stopped doing after his passing. I am making strides while healing day by day!

Like most parents, I prepared Paul for life should something happen to me, but I was not prepared for life should something happen to him. No one prepared me. No one can prepare you for such a loss. I am a work in progress, and I know God is working on me daily. I have learned how to smile again, and I am teaching others it's okay to smile as well. God continues to heal me, so I can help other survivors, families, and friends who are hurting from the loss of their loved ones. God has brought me so far! I am able to celebrate Paul's beautiful life and not dwell on the ugliness of his death. I now understand how God will allow us to go through pain so something new can rise from those ashes. I have realized you never know what life may bring – good or bad, but no matter what, you have to continue fighting and not fall into despair. There is always hope! I am now on a new journey of discovery and I will continue to honor my son as I live my best life, now!

After This

Inspirations by: Julvonnia McDowell

After This...
After this, my imagination has grown beyond comprehension.
Paul was my only son, and I would often say, "It is you and me against the world."
A world filled with so many places and missions.

After This...
I raised Paul to see the beauty in life.
A life overflowing with pure bliss.
He is truly missed.

After This...
A place where you find yourself stuck and seeking a way.
A way in which nothing could prepare this feeling on any given day.
Paul, you were supposed to still be here.
Remember our last conversation?
It still replays over and over in my head.
I am now left with what you last said.

After This....
There is a corner that I keep looking around.
Hoping for something different.
I prepared you if something were to happen to me,
But I never prepared myself if something ever happened to you.
Now I am left to imagine the places you'd go and who you would be.
Pictures are now my forever memory.
I am left to pick up the pieces of what is left of me to ensure the world knows your legacy.

After This....

In Loving Memory:
Paul Sampleton, Jr.

JOURNAL PROMPT

Life is short. Too short for some. We know that everything can change in an instant, and we strive to have gratitude for all the blessings we have. Life is about how you live it and what you do with the time you have. What legacy will you leave behind once you are no longer here?

_____

_____

_____

_____

_____

_____

_____

_____

_____

_____

_____

_____

_____

_____

_____

_____

_____

_____

Photo Credit – Eric Dycus

CHAPTER 4: Author - Falisha Curlin Walker

Falisha S. Curlin Walker is a Christian, wife, mother and hard worker. She received her primary education through Wayne Township school districts in Indianapolis, Indiana. She later received her Certified Nursing Assistant certification, Pharmacy Tech certification and phlebotomy certification.

Falisha married her childhood sweetheart and is the mother of five children.

On May 11, 2019, her son, William Wanyea Walker, age 23, lost his life. He was her oldest son of her five children. His murder broke her down. Darkness and emptiness was her way of living. She learned to lean for God and not to what the devil wanted her to believe. She joined several local groups to help her navigate this new but unwanted journey, including *Purpose4MyPain*. She felt that the women in the group understood the pain and heartache of losing a child. Falisha and William's story has been featured on several local news outlets. This mother is determined to keep her son's name alive by elevating her voice, bringing awareness, and supporting other mothers who are on their journey of grief.

In the near future, Falisha plans to open a community center called M&M, "Mister's Mission", where they will promote violence prevention and intervention by assisting them in learning a trade that can land them a reputable work in their communities and with stable employment, Falisha hopes to keep them away from gun violence and the judicial system.

Falisha's life quote is: Psalms 30:5 - *"Weeping endures for a night, but joy comes in the morning."* Falisha says that she still cries almost every day and night, but she knows that God carries her umbrella. She knows that God picks his strongest soldiers for the toughest battles and realizes that the battle is not really hers, it is the Lord's.

CHAPTER 4: MY UNCHOSEN BATTLE

By
Falisha Curlin Walker

Weeping may endure for a night but joy comes in the morning.
-Psalms 30:5

"*Oh God!! Please, help me!*" The pain that ripped through my stomach was horrible. This is the second time I've had to go to the bathroom and still cannot use it. There was an eerie feeling that had me worried and wondering what was wrong. I checked my phone and laid back down. As I drifted off to sleep, I heard the loud sound of the phone, "Ring, Ring". That is all I heard, and I jumped up and quickly grabbed the phone before it stopped ringing. "*Hello,*" I said. "*Baby, come to the Venus Nightclub,*" said the person on the other end of the phone. I responded "*NO!*" "*Come up here! Mister was shot!!*" I jumped up, confused, scared, wondering who, what, why, how could this happen? I grabbed my gun while talking to myself, "*He must've run out of bullets. Chanyea, get up!*" I frantically yelled, "*Mister got shot, and he must've run out of bullets.*" She jumped up, confused. The other kids woke up, from the commotion I made when yelling, Mister, was shot. "*Momma, can we come,*" they asked. "*No, I'll have somebody pick you up once we get to the hospital.*" Once, I got in the car, I grabbed my chest. "*Mister, fight baby, fight!*"

The drive to the Venus seemed interminable. My mind drifted a thousand times, but the fierce pain I was having was fading away. The eerie feeling in the pit of my stomach was getting the best of me. I arrived at Tibbs and 16th Street near the Venus nightclub amidst flashing lights and yellow tape. I noticed a few cars, but no ambulance. Confusion clouded my mind! *"Damn, this traffic light is long, for no reason,"* I thought. I turned the corner, barely parking, and jumped out of the car. This was the worst night of my life.

As I parked, I thought, *"Mister, must've gotten transported to the hospital."* I noticed my auntie crying and people were holding her up. I was looking for my husband, their dad. I just started walking slowly up to where the police were standing. I stopped dead in my tracks! Yellow, those are the shoes Mister had on. Dead! *"He's dead!"* I yelled! *"Come, here let me talk to you,"* the officer said. As I slowly approached the body, I looked closer, grabbing my chest, *"That's not him!"* I sighed.

Then, I heard somebody yell. *"He's down there."* I went down two or three steps. I noticed his dreads first. I yelled, *"Who killed my baby? Who killed my baby?"* I felt like I was in the Twilight Zone. I'm standing there, but I'm not there at all. The scream that I screamed, was even scary to me. I knew I was screaming, but in the mental and emotional space I was in I wasn't screaming, at all. When I glanced to my right, I saw my daughter running down the street. I approached the officer. *"Excuse me, sir, that's my son back there!"* *"Ma'am,"* he stated, *"we haven't identified the victims, yet."* *"Well, I don't care who you haven't identified! That's my baby, William Walker!!"* The officer walked away, with his head down. *"Give me a minute,"* he said. A tall bald man approached me. *"Ma'am, you have a question about one of the victims?"* *"Well, first off, my son's name is William Walker, and he's the young man lying right there."* He said, *"Yes, the victim in the back is William Walker, age 23, and he is deceased at the scene."* I dropped my head, as my eyes filled with tears. Confused, hurt, and heartbroken, I tried to move but couldn't. Question after question flooded my mind. Was he scared, did he call out for me, did he die alone, or was someone there when he took his last breath? I said, *"Wait a minute, what time did this happen? This lot is too damn empty for a Friday night. And where is his gun?'* The detective tried to calm me down, *"No, I'm not calming down. Where is everybody? I'm from Haughville! There're two dead bodies, and no bystanders standing around trying to be nosy."* The detective said, *"Ma'am, we have excellent video footage, six cameras that caught the whole murder. Your son was killed minutes from exiting his car. He was on his phone when he was wandering around looking like he was searching for someone. Once he approached the edge of the sidewalk, he was ambushed."* *"So, you're telling me he was set up? And the other guy,"* I asked? *"Well,"* the detective stated, *"he is from Chicago, so we were hoping you can help us out. Who did your son deal with from Chicago?"* I replied, *"I don't know. He has one or two friends, and they're not from no damn Chicago."*

I stood there crying. I looked up and said, *"Thank you, God, for the twenty-three years you gave him to me; although they were fleeting, I thank You."* The officer said, *"Are you okay?"* I replied, *"Yes, I'm fine."* Standing there looking at my baby on the ground, I had a million feelings coursing through me. When was the last time I told him I loved him? I was asking God for help because the whole time I was standing there, I never realized I had my gun in my hand! I paced up and down the street and questioned how someone could do my son like this? Was it worth it? I didn't know what to think; how I was going to tell my other kids Mister was gone and never coming back.

The day that that coward took my son, a part of me died too. To bury a child is the worst feeling ever. No one can understand the aftermath of losing a child unless they have experienced it. The pain cuts deep, so deep it reaches the depths of your soul, and it takes you to a place that only God can get you out of.

As I prepared to leave the scene, I watched my son being placed into a white bag and it finally hit me, 'he's never coming back to me!' I couldn't wrap my head around it. Then the coroner told me 'the body needs to be out of the morgue on Monday no later than 9:00 am' which made me start crying all over again. I didn't have the first clue what funeral home I needed to call, what arrangements needed to be made, etc. I was coming up with nothing – only a blank mind. I felt lost, but I felt myself nod in acknowledgment. I drove home in an awkward silence while trying to put things together of how my life had changed forever that night.

I remember walking around the mall, crying as I picked out the items Mister would need. It seemed so foreign because I had to accept that my son was dead and gone. I got everything and headed home. People came and sat with me when it happened, and I received telephone calls, but nothing helped the pain. While attempting to grasp the finality of it all and put my life in some kind of perspective, I finalized his arrangements. My son was gone, gone forever. I didn't want to talk, eat, or sleep; I could barely function. I wanted my son back and I wanted him back, right now!

On the day of my son's funeral, I went to the church and all I could do was cry. I questioned God and thought, "*Why did I have to be chosen for this battle?*" "*God, I'm not strong enough, I need my son. He didn't even get to experience fatherhood, nothing!*" The service was short, or did it seem that way? I remember at the end of the service, the director said, "*Dad and Mom, come on, so we can close the casket.*" My husband went up to the casket, bent his head down, and then told me to fold the blankets. I folded the blankets as if Mister was a baby going home for the first time. That memory made me cry out, "*No, I can't because he's not going home. This is so unfair! Why my child??? WHY MY CHILD???*"

WHY MY CHILD?

I know you're not supposed to question God, but I'm lost, confused, and heartbroken. My faith in God has me conflicted. I need to know why, but I'm struggling because my faith will not allow me to ask why. I know we were born to die, but why did he have to go so soon? As I looked at my baby lying on the ground, I felt helpless. I remember asking the officer to cover him up. He heartlessly replied; "*he can't feel it.*" I yelled back, "*I can!*" "*This is unfair. No one deserves to be left on the freezing ground.*" Without permission, my mind drifted to a place of darkness, unnatural to humanity.

Journal Entry #1; 05/11/2019 - *I got the worst call ever, that my son was shot. My first reaction was he ran out of bullets. I reached into the closet on the top shelf and grabbed my handgun. While driving to the Venus Nightclub, I kept telling myself "he's okay." Once I realized he's gone, I'm speechless, however, my mind is going a mile a minute asking, "where's his gun?" Then my mind switches gears and asks, "Where's everybody at?" "How in the HELL did they catch him slipping!!!" My eyes filled with tears, while my heart was breaking. "Mister what happened, baby!!!" I began the blame game and blamed myself for being too damn tired, and how me being exhausted cost you, your life. My heart feels nothing but revenge. I'm going to kill everyone who did this. You took my child and now you will pay with your life or your children's life! PERIOD!*

I'm standing there waiting for the coroner to pick up his body. I feel the coldness in my blood, my heart was no longer beating red, it was black as a panther hunting in the desert, chasing his prey. How can you do this to me, to him?? May God have mercy on their soul, especially when I find out who did this to my Mister. God help me! This pain is so unfair. Why did God choose me, my kids, my world? My thoughts, poor. My heartbeat, irregular. All I can do is scream; I need you JESUS!!!! Help me through this, I don't think I can adjust to this new normal. All of that was racing through my brain, as I drifted off to sleep only to be awakened by my phone ringing! "Hello, is it true?" the caller asked. "Is what true, Mister being killed? Yes!" I replied in irritation! "You sure!" they responded. "Look here, don't ask me no questions and my son is dead and gone!" was my final response before hanging up the phone.

Journal Entry #7; 05/20/2020 - *Now that the services are done, I cannot believe my son is gone. Tears are coming nonstop. My heart is hurting badly, and my appetite is gone. I need answers!! How do I go on knowing you're no longer here? Why does it hurt? Why can't I sleep? Nothing but silence, I am not receiving any answers. Why haven't there been any arrests, especially since there were six videos? I am left with more questions than answers. I hate the police; I have no answers and no updates on the investigation. Especially, since they said the videos were clear as day. Mister, I promise, you will not be another unsolved murder, no matter what!!! Period. I know what it is, you're not their child, so they don't care. But they had me all the way messed up, seriously. I know for damn sure if it was their child, all of Haughville would've been shut down. All they saw was two more black men dead at the hands of another black man. This was crazy! Every time I write in the journal it makes your death so much harder. I love you son, no matter what, you're forever my MISTER 23#.*

'Nights seem so much longer now; I know I'm not sleeping but, how could I?' The sound of someone knocking on the door took me out of my daydream. "*How can I help you?*" I said after opening the door. "*I'm a reporter from Fox 59,*" they replied. "*Ok and?*" was my response. "*Did you know the person who killed your son was apprehended?*" the reporter said. "*When?*" I anxiously asked. "*Well, the report says, Monday.*" I was thrilled and lost at the same time. Why haven't the detectives reached out? The reporter then says, "*he was apprehended, not far from your house. At the time of the young man's arrest, he had a handgun, drugs, and not to mention, he had cut off his home detention monitor.*" Tears began flowing nonstop, 'why did this coward kill my baby,' I thought. Anger took over me again and I wanted to strangle him, whoever he is, with my bare hands.

I was caught up in my own thoughts, when I heard the reporter say, "*tell me about William, who was he?*" With a smile in my voice, I said, "*he was a generous and lovable person. He was my son, my young king, who didn't have the opportunity to experience everything life has to offer. But, to the public eye, he was just another young man dead by gun violence.*" After talking with the reporter. I decided to call the detective. "*Hello, detective, this is Falisha, William Walker's mother. It was brought to my attention that my son's killer was arrested. I was wondering why you haven't reached out to give me an update and why I had to hear about the arrest from Fox 59 news who's airing the story on the 6:00 clock news?*" He stated rudely and nastily, "*Look, this isn't the First*

*F****ing 48!!! We don't solve crimes in two damn days."* I lost it! I screamed into the phone, *"How can you speak to me like that?"* I said, *"If it was your damn child, you wouldn't be saying that."* I said, *"You'll reap what you sow."* as I slammed down my phone.

Journal Entry #24 - *How can people be so rude? How dare he use that language with me. As I'm writing, I'm calling him every name in the book; but a child of God. Lord, I need You. These thoughts racing through my head are positively awful. No one understands how I feel. I can't move, I'm stuck, and no one cares. Daily, I feel like I am drawn deeper and deeper into the dark. I hate getting up, I hate people, I hate everything that makes me feel like this. Then to think, my mother went to the media and did a whole story on my son as if I weren't in the picture. Instead of her holding my hand, all she thought about was putting her name with my son's. I wonder, how long is my body supposed to be numb? This feeling is unnatural. I need to seek help for myself as well as my family. We are all so lost, dear GOD???*

I received a call from my cousin-in-law, and he was having a "Classic Bowl" for Mothers Against Gun Violence. This event was to bring awareness to mothers who lost a child or who have been impacted by violence. So, he gave me the number to a lady who runs a support group. I called her, and we talked for a couple of hours. I knew mentally I wasn't alone and someone else knew how I was feeling. I was excited to meet other mothers and hear their stories of how they went through the struggle, too.

When I first met this group of ladies, I was like a kid in a candy store. Listening to their stories and crying and thinking, *"Damn, this is heartbreaking. So many of us mothers are hurting due to the gun violence in our city."* As I became more transparent when sharing my story, the more I felt at ease. The group Purpose4MyPain has helped me to recognize something in me I haven't seen in a long while.

Yes, I now have a purpose. That purpose is to bring awareness to my son, his life, and his death so that his name will be more significant than a number in a file cabinet. I planned to organize a community center in his honor, calling it "M&M Mister's Mission". Yes, Mister William Walker's life had a purpose and will continue to have a purpose.

In Loving Memory:
William Wanyea Walker

JOURNAL PROMPT

I remember walking up to the scene and seeing the yellow tape. I realized my child was dead and gone. All I could do was look up at the sky, and say "Thank you God! For giving me the twenty-three years you gave "Mister" to us."

If you were in a midst of a storm would you be able to say thank you God?

_____

_____

_____

_____

_____

_____

_____

_____

_____

_____

_____

_____

_____

_____

Photo Credit – Eric Dycus

CHAPTER 5: Author - Valeria Horton

Valeria Horton is an Army veteran who currently resides in Marion, Indiana. She works for the government as a budget analyst. Ms. Horton is the founder of Jayva's Love Foundation Inc., a non-profit organization. Valeria is a certified mediator and mentor coach. She loves to travel and has lived in places including Kuwait and Korea. She plans to live in Portmore, Jamaica where she has a home built. In her free time, she loves to spend time with family. Jayva was her only biological child who has passed, but for some reason kids love her. Valeria has a bachelor's degree in Forensic Accounting and a minor in Auditing.

CHAPTER 5: JAYVA'S LEGACY: A MIRACLE TO A BLESSING

By

Valeria Horton

"Grief - It is hard to understand what is a dream and what is reality. You wander around daydreaming, misinterpreting what is real."
-Valeria Horton

It took years for Jayva to get here, only for her to be taken away at such an early age. Through her life journey, and after she was gone; three concepts have guided me through my grief journey and my life: faith, forgiveness, and following my life's purpose. Sometimes God speaks to us even when we are not ready to listen. It takes a lot to hear and understand what God is telling you. He's saying: *"How strong is your faith in Me?"* I know I hadn't been a faithful nor religious person, but I believe God always has a plan for us, and sometimes it takes a tragedy for us to hear Him. *"My child, you must forgive to heal."* One of the steps in healing is to forgive. When and how you forgive is unique to each person, but to move on, you must forgive. Holding on to hatred, anger, and bitterness only brings dis-ease. *"Are you ready to fulfill your purpose that I have planned out for you?"* While you go through life trying to find your true purpose, sometimes you may never know what that is until tragedy strikes. I found my life's purpose after Jayva's death.

The life of Jayva M. Horton was nothing short of a miracle, a true blessing from God. In over ten years, I attempted many fertility options (from pills to shots) and nothing; no scares, no possibilities - nothing. My last option before seeking a surrogate was to do In Vitro Fertilization (IVF). I did one round of IVF and stopped due to the cost. After that round of IVF, I had given up all hope and options for having a child. At the age of thirty-five, I felt useless! The one thing in life I wanted most was to be a mother. As a part of Jayva's legacy, I continue to raise and care for many children, but nothing compared to having my own.

Faith...

In early 2011, a young woman I knew was pregnant, and she did not want the baby. At the time, she knew I wanted to have a child. We talked, and she agreed to give me her baby, but as with many things in life, plans change. She changed her mind. It wasn't to be. This was devastating to me! It was out of my control.

In March 2012, I was having some symptoms that made me question if I was actually pregnant. Although I had nothing to compare it to, I decided to take a pregnancy test. While I waited for the results, many thoughts went through my mind. When you have taken so many pregnancy tests and wanted nothing more than to get a positive result, you have doubts and you do not want to get your hopes up, only to be let down. Well, the time was up, and it was time to get the results: PREGNANT! At first, I thought this must be a mistake, I was excited and speechless, yet nervous and unsure, simultaneously! At this point, I discerned God does answer prayers.

I would love to say the pregnancy was uncomplicated and went well, but that wasn't my truth. Jayva fought hard to be here and went through many trials and tribulations, none God said I couldn't handle. During my first trimester, I was at work and started bleeding. I left work and went to the Emergency Room (ER). At the ER, all they could say was that since I was in my first trimester it was possible that I was miscarrying and there was nothing they could do. All I felt was sadness, fear, and hurt! I went home for some bed rest and waited to see what God had planned. By His grace, she reached full term and was delivered on December 2, 2012. Jayva was my happy and healthy bundle of joy!

The first six months of Jayva's life went fine until the day I came home from work and took her upstairs. I was holding her and out of the blue she took a deep breath, and her body went limp in my arms. I rushed her to the Emergency Room, which was about five minutes away. When we arrived at the ER, and she was lying on the table, she acted her normal self, as if nothing ever happened. The doctor examined her and kept her for a twenty-four-hour observation. We were told from the test results, they could see she'd been unresponsive, but couldn't tell why. I was frustrated, I felt like the doctors should have told us more. I asked, *"God, why do I feel like I am being punished?"* Over the years other incidents tested my faith. One time she had a serious burn on her foot. Another time, Jayva was involved in a car accident, but thankfully she was not injured. Every time something like that happened, all I could do was think, *"God, why are you testing my faith?"*

The last incident took place on August 24, 2017. Jayva was four years, eight months, and twenty-two days old. We were at my cousin Shammeka's house. The children were home from school, playing outside. It was a bright, warm, and sunny day. Jayva was playing on a riding toy in the driveway which was on a hill that she could ride down. There was a van at the top of the driveway, well out of the way from all the children. As fate would have it, one of the children got into the van and somehow put the van in neutral. The van rolled down the driveway and traveled the same path Jayva took while riding the toy. She was oblivious to the approaching danger. To my horror, the van rolled over Jayva! All I heard was, *"Momma!"* I didn't know it was Jayva yelling with the noise from all the children who were playing outside.

It never occurred to me, God would punish me by hurting my only child, or so I thought. Whatever fog I was in, it quickly cleared, and I realized it was Jayva who called for me. I moved into 'Mommy protection mode' and snatched Jayva out of the way before the van could drive over her again. I moved her from the street to the grass. I talked to her and laid next to her. She seemed to be okay. It seemed like she may have had a broken femur, but she was coherent. We said her name, we recited her ABCs, and she was counting. While talking with Jayva, I called 911. While the dispatcher sent help, we kept her engaged until the ambulance arrived. After what seemed like an eternity, the ambulance took us to the hospital. On the way to the hospital, I believed Jayva was fine. I didn't believe her condition was serious nor anything she couldn't heal from. Once we arrived at the local hospital, the doctors decided to airlift her to another hospital via the helicopter (lifeline). We drove to the hospital, while Jayva was being life-lined. When we arrived at the new hospital we were escorted to another room, and the doctor sent for the chaplain. I stopped dead in my tracks, I knew something was not right. The doctor informed us this was a standard operating procedure when a patient is admitted via helicopter. The chaplain joined us in the room and delivered the news. Jayva's heart stopped in route, and she passed away.

I was in shock, my mind and heart stopped, and I was glued to the spot I was in. My body took over while my mind shut down. I was in denial. I kept thinking, *"My baby is not dead! God's gift to me and the world is not gone!"* At that moment I heard God say, *"Trust Me, I will never give you anything you cannot handle. Continue to keep your faith in Me and I will show you what I have planned for you."*

How can I move forward with my life, and remain strong while showing the least number of emotions to the outside world? As I took this journey with God, nights were the hardest, and when I broke down the most, crying enough tears that could fill an ocean. The pain was so palpable I felt it in my chest and my body. There were many times I didn't want to get out of my bed. I only wanted to join my child. My mind knew it wasn't right, but my heart was broken. The silence in our home was deafening. I missed the laughter and youthful energy that was a constant in our home causing it to become a cold and lonely place. I now know how it feels to be lonely while surrounded by friends and loved ones. My life and my home will never be the same! It's devastating to lose your child, your only child, and the gift God gave to both you and the world.

Whenever I feel depressed and lonely, I talk to God and say, "*God are you trying to test my faith?*" In response, I hear God saying, "*Valeria, I have sent you many warnings to let you know that I am real. I let you know that I will come back to get what I lent to you, which is your child. She has served her purpose here on earth, now it is time for her to be with me, and you to live your purpose. You may not know what it is, but you have shown me your faith in Me is strong.*"

Forgiveness

The first thing God revealed to me after Jayva passed, was the gift of forgiveness. I realized I could forgive even if I didn't forget, which began my forgiveness journey. God never allowed me to indulge in hate or anger. I never blamed the parents of the little girl who caused the accident with the van. I understood things happen that we have no control over and that's why they are called accidents. Many people may never understand how I can still talk to them or still have them in my life. I know this is hard on them, especially the mother, Lakeiah (Kia), like it is on me. It doesn't benefit either of us to hate or be angry with each other. God taught me to heal is to forgive. Our healing began when Kia asked to do Jayva's hair for her funeral. I allowed her to not only prepare Jayva's hair but to also do mine as well. I realized that this was one of the most challenging experiences for us both. I also made myself available for her to talk whenever the opportunity presented itself. This assisted us in our healing process. Most importantly, I let her know that I do not blame her or her daughter for any of this. Kia has always been my hairdresser, and I continued that relationship – until the end of January 2021 when Kia unexpectedly passed away. Before the incident, we had a close relationship. Jayva loved to go over to Kia's house to play with her kids, especially when I was getting my hair done.

God said to me, "*I have given you a child for a reason.*" When God comes back to take your child, it is one of the hardest things for a parent to understand. While we believe we should live longer than our kids, that is not always God's plan. That child had a purpose here on earth. While we may never discover or understand what a child's purpose might be, that purpose may be revealed after they are gone. Tomorrow is not promised to anyone, so it is important to experience life each day as if it were your last; we never know when God calls His children home.

Follow Your Purpose

While she is not here on earth, Jayva's legacy continues to bless others. She was my greatest blessing and the revealer of my life's purpose. Like many others, my purpose introduced itself during my darkest hours, and I have to give God all the credit. I never expected any of this, nor do I know how to communicate how it all started. While trudging around in a daze, functioning off of faith, and relying on God's guidance, I started a non-profit organization called Jayva's Love Foundation, Inc. Through the burial process, I didn't realize the cost of burying my angel nor the cost of the headstone. While thinking about my experience, I realized many families cannot afford to pay for their loved one's burial without help from a 'Go-Fund Me' account. Even with the 'Go Fund Me' account, families fail to ask for enough money, and many children are left at the cemetery with no headstone (unknown). While we cannot provide financial assistance, we do provide a temporary memorial marker for families who have lost a child under the age of twenty-one who cannot afford a headstone. This allows for families to have a temporary marker at their child's gravesite, or they use it for a memorial garden. Jayva's Love Foundation, Inc.'s mission is to ensure "No Angel Is Left Unknown." Jayva's legacy continues as I became the voice and used the strength God has given me to be a strong example to others. Through Jayva's death, I have been able to listen to others who have experienced this pain. I am not trained nor educated in grief counseling, but I do have personal experience. While many people say, "*I feel your pain,*" they don't, the loss of a child is painful and can become even harder when you don't have other children or are unable to have any more. One of the other ways Jayva's legacy continues, is through showing others how walking in God's faith, can take you further in life than hate and anger. We serve an awesome God, a God who does not make mistakes. We may hurt and never understand, however, we need to learn and accept tomorrow is not promised for anyone. This is true for any age from the time of conception to old age.

Grief isn't designed to be easy! We all go through the many stages of grief. What worked for me may not work for someone else. I never imagined how my faith in God would be tested, and I'd learn my strength is God-given! It was that strength that led me to the forgiveness that healed me and gave me the courage to move forward in life. It showed me the importance of experiencing God's light of love rather than the darkness and negativity of hurt, hate, and/or pain one can drown in when grieving. Finding my life's purpose was a gift from God I am truly blessed to have and to work on. Your purpose may come from a tragedy, but you have the power to turn your tragedy into a triumph. God has given each of us a purpose. It is up to us to discover what it is. One day we all have to die and when the time comes, are you going to be ready? I am grateful to my Horton family who are always supporting me.

To find out more about Jayva's Love Foundation, Inc. you can follow us on Facebook and Instagram under Jayva's Love Foundation, Inc. Our website is www.Jayvaslove.com.

In Loving Memory:
Jayva M. Horton

JOURNAL PROMPT

Losing your child is hard but losing your only child is different kind of test in faith. In what ways can you relate to my chapter? Write down ways that you are learning to forgive yourself and others? Write down what you hear that God is telling you and from a tragedy do you have a triumph?

_____

_____

_____

_____

_____

_____

_____

_____

_____

_____

_____

_____

_____

_____

_____

_____

_____

Photo Credit – Calvin Wayne Photography

CHAPTER 6: Author - Olga Williams

Olga Williams is a Savannah, Georgia native. She is a successful entrepreneur, dynamic speaker, and emcee. She is an author, and inspirer of all things LOVE. She enjoys being a wife to her husband and a mother, always remembering the importance of creating memories with family. One of Olga's businesses is Icons Hair Studio & Boutique. A hair salon that is not your average hair salon. Olga quickly realized that God had given her a gift of VOICE that inspired women from not just behind the salon chair. Olga's unique style of emceeing has paved the way for numerous events both locally and nationally.

Olga became an advocate of gun violence prevention when her seventeen-year-old bonus son Dominique was killed intentionally by a fifteen-year old. It began her next chapter on the journey of inspiring and motivating other families. She is using her voice to get in the fight to end gun violence. She is a volunteer Gun Violence Prevention Advocate with a grassroots organization. Olga is also co-founder of Dominique's World, an organization that collaborates with mentoring groups to INSPIRE, EMPOWER and IGNITE communities around the world. Her organization host an annual all male fashion show, Bow Ties and Blazers that honors the lives stolen by gun violence and celebrates living sons.

Olga's inspiration of all things Love, led her and her husband Leroy to create "Couples Only" a date night experience for married and engaged couples to remember the significance of why they LOVE.

CHAPTER 6: YOU DIDN'T GROW UNDER MY HEART, BUT IN IT

By

Olga Williams

"Not flesh of my flesh, nor bone of my bone, but still miraculously my own."
-Anonymous

I met Leroy in November 1998, and he was undeniably charming and handsome. So charming, that the day we met we laughed and talked for hours as if we had known each other for years. A friendship evolved instantly because there was something so loving and compassionate about him, and I needed to know exactly where this was going. We began dating, the usual movies, playing pool, and dinner, but Leroy's attentiveness, wanting to be a part, and being interested in my life hooked me. I knew he had children, but I had only met his daughters, TiBreau and Roleiah. They were the cutest and most mannerable young ladies.

Leroy was from South Carolina and I lived in Georgia, but it was only about twenty-five minutes away. Leroy had the girls a lot on Saturday afternoons, and they would come over with him from time to time when he would visit. One afternoon, the summer of 1999, Leroy and his friends came by the salon where I was a Hairstylist. I was working, and he brought his son, this tiny cute little baby named Dominique. It did not take Dominique long to get to know me and his unknown surroundings; he wandered around the shop with confidence. He was so adorable. Leroy had already talked so much about him, and he was just as cute as Leroy described. Ironically, it was not until five years later, that Dominique would join Leroy for a visit. I had briefly moved to Charlotte, North Carolina, and had just returned to Savannah. At that time, Dominique was older, much more talkative, and inquisitive. He asked me so many questions as if I was being interrogated.

I remember cooking manwiches during one of his visits, with doughnuts for dessert. I helped him with his schoolwork, and we watched television. I tried to keep him entertained as best I could because I had no children of my own, only younger cousins who always wanted to be at my house - the funhouse they called it. As the evening ended, Dominique asked me, "Can I call you Momma Lo?" I can remember that day so clearly because I was not expecting him to say that. For me, it was strange that we laughed and simply brushed it off as if that weren't a monumental moment in our relationship. I thought it was a sweet gesture. I never imagined I would actually be his Momma Lo when his daddy and I married, five years later.

Dominique was ten when his father and I got married. He lived in South Carolina, about thirty minutes away from us. He would come to Georgia to visit on weekends, or when my family would have celebrations, birthday parties, family reunions, or simply playing video games with my nephews or cousins. As with many blended families, we don't use the word 'step.' Dominique was family and my family welcomed him the same. Dominique was a lot like his Dad, charming, friendly, and loved to talk. Of his greatest loves in life, playing the drums and dancing topped the list. An art his father had taught him, and he had perfected. Dominique had so much skill that he was on-demand to perform not only at his church but other local churches in the low country of South Carolina.

A year after we got married, I was expecting a baby girl and Dominique was so excited! He often joked about dressing her in the latest sneakers and polos from his love for clothes and shoes. When Lindsay was born, she was premature, and Dominique would tell me how he was going to be the best big brother and bodyguard. Which turned out to be a true statement. As she grew older, Dominique was right there on the weekends, holidays, and birthdays when he would visit and was always looking out for his "Sis" as he called her.

I remember the exact day that Dominique changed from coming on the weekends to living with us permanently. He entered the front door and had tons and tons of clothes and said, "*Momma Lo,*" as he called me, "*What's for dinner?*" The next year and a half were filled with memories, memories, and more memories – many with Lindsay, Dominique, and me, because Leroy's job required him to travel over the road. He would mostly be home on the weekends. School drop-offs, football and basketball practice, teacher conferences, and evenings of homework and band, were a few of our rituals. Not to mention dinners full of Lindsay and Dominique laughing, joking, and simply having fun.

Dominique was always right there to help his Lil' Sis with anything she demanded of him. He never forgot he promised to be her bodyguard, and with their eleven-year age difference you would believe he would want his little sister to leave him alone, but that was not the case with this brother-sister duo, their bond was incredibly close. When it came to what Dominique taught me, there were countless SNAP CHAT videos, selfie tutorials, and everything fashion. We attended Wednesday night bible study and Dominique would tell me, "*Momma Lo, that drummer was aw'ight, but when I get my chance on those drums, I am gonna show out in here.*" He was telling the truth.

I had literally gone from weekend mom to everyday Bonus Mom, so much so that I was nominated by the teachers at Dominique's school and became President of the PTA. I remember dropping Dominique off the first day at his new school and him telling me I could not escort him in or give him a kiss, after dropping Lindsay off for her first day of kindergarten. We joked about dropping him off far enough from the front door that's acceptable with him being the new kid on the block. He called/text several times that day to tell me he was fine at his new school and for me to stop worrying. I guess he could sense it, because I wanted this to go so well for him.

I love creating moments and having a wonderful time, but there were goals that Dominique and I had set when he came to live with us. We would have conversations about what he wanted in his life and his future. Dominique knew that there were two things he wanted: to be in his correct grade and to play sports at his new High School. His future goal was to be a famous drummer like the iconic Tony Royster Jr. He worked diligently that school year, attending after-school programs and getting any tutorial opportunities that we could find. He had thrived at his new school, joined mentor programs, the band, and played sports.

Thanksgiving rolled around, then Christmas and the New Year! I remember while journaling my New Year's Resolution for 2015, I said to God I'd be thankful for strength, love, and the ability to uplift others, and promising God I would have gratitude for all things. The year started off great, I was blessed with a new business location, Lindsay had started "big girl school," Dominique was halfway through his tenth-grade year of high school, and Leroy was finding his groove in the logistics world. Everything was going GREAT! However, I never imagined how everything I had written in my journal was what I needed to take me, not only through the New Year's resolutions I'd made, but would be the sustaining force as my life changed forever. The seven months of intentional daily writing brought me where I am five years later, and through one of the greatest losses imaginable.

Friday, July 10, 2015, Dominique turned seventeen and spent that evening with his mom. The following day he was back home, and we went to Beaufort, South Carolina, to attend a surprise birthday party for my father-in-love's mother. Dominique never wanted to miss a family get-together. After the party, Lindsay wanted to go with her Grannie and little cousins, so Leroy, Dominique, and I rode back home to Georgia. The ride home was a lot different; he was speaking about how much he loved his son and how he always wanted Dominique to know that he would always have his best interest at heart. He shared his philosophy on friendships, when he told Dominique he needed to always be careful when selecting his friends. Something about that conversation seemed different, although it was the same Leroy physically, he was different spiritually and emotionally.

The next day, Sunday, Dominique was leaving for five days to play drums at "The SC State Congress of Christian Education Convention." When Dominique got his clothes together and his drumsticks, he reminded me he was going to set the conference off with his drumming skills and fashion! He gave me a hug and a quick kiss on the cheek. I never considered when he left out of the door, the same door he always entered yelling, *"Momma Lo, what's for dinner?"* would become a memory of him walking out that door for the last time. Dominique had returned from the trip that Friday and was spending time with his mom in Hilton Head, South Carolina, and later hung out with some friends when there was an altercation.

Two days after the altercation, Sunday, July 19, 2015, Dominique was murdered! He was killed by a fifteen-year-old in an intentional act of violence. It was a senseless act of gun violence that altered the life journey I believed I was on. I was bathing Lindsay when Leroy called and I remember, repeatedly asking him, *"Gone where?"* when he said, *"Dominique is gone!"* I heard the distress and sorrow in his voice as I was pacing back and forth from the kitchen to the bathroom where I was bathing Lindsay. I was so distraught that I left my daughter in the tub by herself. I was in despair. This is unbelievable, devastating doesn't compare to how I was feeling. This cannot be real.

I went through the motions with Dominique's mom going to the funeral home, picking out a casket, and putting a program together. Even mustering up enough strength to speak at the funeral, comforting my daughters and my husband, comforting his classmates, and attending ceremonies in his honor, all while grieving myself. He was so loved and there were so many memorials. There was a tree dedicated in his honor in Savannah, Georgia, senior night recognition at the high school football game, and a drum recognition at the Baptist Church. Dominique was LOVED. I found myself correcting people when they said, *"Sorry for your loss"* because Dominique was not lost, he was murdered, never returning to say, *"Pops, Sis or Momma Lo"* again.

I still had to be a wife to a man who had been robbed of his only son who was set to carry on his last name for generations to come. We were struggling with Dominique's death, and while reminiscing one day my husband said *"...a piece of me died that day."* To make it even more challenging, my five-year-old daughter was questioning why God isn't answering her prayers, especially since we've always told her *"...God answers prayers."* Her limited knowledge led her to say, *"...if we die right now, we can see Dominique again."* She couldn't grasp the fact that Dominique wasn't ever coming home again. There were times when I would go past her room and hear her talking to Dominique asking him when he's coming back? It was on those days that everything hurt, and nothing made sense. I kept searching and quickly learned there's no right way to grieve. Oftentimes, I found myself secretly crying because I thought it wasn't healthy for Leroy and Lindsay to witness.

When you love someone, that is beautiful! When they die unexpectedly and as horrifically as Dominique did, the pain is unimaginable! I had to remind myself Dominique did not simply die HE WAS MURDERED! This tragedy was my inspiration to begin journaling again. It's the one thing I had stopped doing that always made me feel empowered. I remember writing one day, "*the darker the situation was, the brighter my light would have to shine. God placed me here so now I needed to be the light.*" As I began to pray and journal, I realized Dominique's life was not brief, but he lived a long full life, filled with love by, and for, so many. I needed to pray for love, and I needed to understand that I LOVE life; the good, the bad, and the ugly! I had to remind myself that God gave me the strength and courage to endure, and I needed to access that strength daily. I realized that the pain my family was experiencing had to be a pain that other families, whose loved ones were murdered, were enduring. I knew that Dominique's death was not in vain, it taught me there's purpose in my pain.

I needed to start a movement - a movement where telling Dominique's story, could change the hearts of young people and/or help a father/mother realize their children's life matters. A platform that would allow me to show the world our children are blessings, our greatest loves, and their lives matter. One that would allow me to speak into the hearts and minds of Stepmoms to teach them the importance of being Bonus Moms.

On Dominique's eighteenth birthday, we invited some family and friends over to announce our plans to launch "Dominique's World." Dominique's World is a non-profit that INSPIRES youth to dream big and provides them with the tools to attain their goals while EMPOWERING them to build self-confidence and self-worth. It's a place where our youth's full potential can be IGNITED from their passion. What I learned from Dominique's life, accomplishments and death are: there's no STRENGTH that can prepare you for this journey, I had to swim and not drown in my grief or the unfairness I was experiencing, I had to be a FIRE and a LIGHT for others, and there's no such thing as too much love for a child. When God assigned me this journey, He knew I was going to use everything in me to be a voice for Dominique, youth, and other families going through what we've gone through.

Can You Hear The Drum?

Can you hear the beat that goes on and on with a melody so sweet
It beats nonstop like our heartbeat.
The Grace that this drummer carries.
The sound that sends vibrations through and through
Can you hear the drum?
Can you hear the sound to the cadence of peace?
A sound that now rocks me to sleep.
A sound I now hear as a memory.
Dominique, I hear the beat.
Can you hear the drum?
The sound that now beats within me
I stop and get in tune with the beat
Our drummer is forever
A sound I can hear from Heaven
Through the clouds, raindrops and sunshine
A drummer whose beats always makes me smile
Can you hear the drum?

In Loving Memory
Dominique Xavier Milton Williams

JOURNAL PROMPT

Trusting God for me means praying and asking God to always order my steps, even when I can't lift my foot to even start the first step. Finding courage, building my strength, and knowing how to accept my assignment changed my life. Please use this journal to share how you turned your journey of pain into PURPOSE. Remember, we all have a story...... GRATITUDE.

Photo Credit – Eric Dycus

CHAPTER 7: Author - Thomasena Colbert

Thomasena Colbert is an Indiana native, who is debuting as an author in this Anthology Beautiful Resilience. After suffering, first-hand, the tragic loss and murder of her son Isaiah Horton, Thomasena's world was turned upside down as she suddenly found herself in a whirlwind of confusion and sadness. Her career, which was at it's peak, came to a complete halt, and her life was at a standstill, like she had just been placed on another planet. Just barely peeling herself out of bed, on most days, losing Isaiah helped her tap into another realm of reality, one that helped her emerge into a different kind of woman; a woman who now has two heartbeats instead of one.

Unsure of which way to turn, Thomasena discovered that healing is a process that is not meant to be forced or rushed. She drew her strength from her personal relationship with Christ, her husband, her children. She cherishes friendships, as well as taking nature walks with her family dog, Jacob. She also found herself attending small groups at Heartland Church, where she fellowships. The small groups that she is a part of include *Purpose4MyPain, Purposeful Living Inc.* and *Moms Demand Action.*

After losing her son, her job and even her desire to live again, Thomasena picked herself up and began to re-evaluate her life and think about what truly mattered. She surrendered to God and allowed her tragedy to push her into the next phase of the healing process. She knew she wanted to help families in similar situations, so she established a nonprofit called What Elephant, inc., (in honor of Isaiah). Through her pain, she found her purpose and now believes that she is walking that purpose out into the world one person at a time. Today, Thomasena has a loving and supporting husband, Darryl G. Colbert and is the mother of two handsome sons (one of which is a bonus son) three beautiful daughters (another bonus daughter). She enjoys being a 'Big Momma' to nine magnificent grandchildren. She also loves line dancing, listening to music, cooking, and values spending time with her family and friends, especially over a home cooked meal.

CHAPTER 7: AND THEN IT HAPPENED TO ME

By

Thomasena Colbert

Healing is more than surviving a storm, healing is acknowledging the storm and showing one another pieces of the readiness plan that worked for you.
                                                        -Thomasena Colbert

God whispered to me for eighteen months to get up. So many days I heard His whisper but didn't move. It was close to Christmas, 1993 in the dead of winter. I was eighteen years old and twenty-nine weeks pregnant with my second son. I was at my cousin's house, which just so happened to be next door to my mom's home. The home I grew up in, attended high school, and where I would graduate from eight months after the birth of my son, Isaiah Dakeem Ali Horton.

Watch out world, here I come! My baby was coming into the world seven weeks early. I was rushed to our little community hospital, where they advised my mother I would need to be transported to the hospital in the state's capital. As I rode in the ambulance, I wasn't in any pain; simply anxious and afraid. I was a young and inexperienced mother. I did not know what to expect. I was a baby, having a baby. When I arrived at the hospital, I was immediately rushed to the emergency room, and the nurses began to hook me up to heart and oxygen monitors and put IVs in my arm. My water had already broken, before arriving at the hospital. My amniotic fluid was depleted, and I was faced with having a dry birth.

I was admitted to the hospital with high hopes the doctors could keep my baby in my womb for the remaining seven weeks. A nearly impossible fete considering my current medical condition and the risk of infection that would put both my life and the baby's life in danger. I was in the hospital for two weeks when the doctor came in and said it was time. He immediately stopped the medications, and the contractions started coming harder and closer together. I had been in labor the entire time I'd been in the hospital. We were at a critical point in my pregnancy because my baby could no longer survive in my womb. My young mind had trouble grasping the severity of the situation, and more importantly, the details of the life and death situation both myself and my baby were facing. I was eighteen, scared, and felt so alone, even though my eldest cousin stood by my side while my mother came as often as her work schedule would permit.

The night of January 22, 1994, the doctors prepared me for surgery; giving me an epidural (that's another story for another time), and four hours later I gave birth to a screaming baby boy, which I named Isaiah after his older brother Isaac. He was a rich, shiny, beautiful Hershey's chocolate color, like his mother, and long like his father. His lungs weren't fully developed, and he remained in the hospital under the doctor's care to allow his lungs to fully develop. Although he was at 6.7 lbs., the doctors wanted him to gain more weight. The level of fear I spoke of previously became an immobilizing fear! Here I am a small-town girl in an unknown city with a new baby. We had been in the hospital for weeks, in a city that's not our home, where I found myself staying with my family after my release, and going back and forth to the hospital to spend time with the precious life that fought his way into this world.

Five years later, Isaiah had grown into a humorous, sweet, rough, tough, and tumbling little guy. Yes, he was all those things. That boy was exasperating and busy. He was the son that loved his mamma and always wanted me to be okay. My immaturity and lack of experience made me think I needed to work towards better provisions, and after a while, I realized only part of that was true. I was taking college courses, which took up almost all my time while I raised my children and worked for companies that offered tuition assistance. My efforts to better myself and the opportunities available to me took me away from my children more than I liked. On my days off, and when not in class, I attempted to be present as much as possible in their lives.

I got so frustrated with his antics at school, especially when he talked and played as if the teacher was interrupting "his day." I was emotionally exhausted, and didn't have the strength or mental capacity to help us both cope. Regardless of how much trouble he got in, I never failed to hug my children daily and tell them how proud I am of them, even when I didn't feel it nor feel like it.

Being a young, single mother, I would be frustrated when I didn't understand some of that energy needed an outlet. I unfortunately did not have the resources and did not have the village I was raised with to jump in and be there for me to afford my children the opportunities I had. Even as a young mother, I was not interested in giving ADD medicine (Adderall) to a child whose body hadn't fully developed, and run the risk of the medication changing the chemical dynamics of his five-year-old mind. He was full of life, loved to draw, spit rhymes (rap), play outside, get dirty, play video games, and play basketball. He was a member, like his mother and uncles, of the Boys and Girls Club (we affectionately called the "club"), and he attended their afterschool program as much as possible. The director took a special liking to Isaiah, his older brother, Isaac, and several other boys from our neighborhood. He was an active child who played hard and worked even harder. He loved riding his bike and hanging out with his cousins.

As a recent high school graduate with no college scholarship opportunities, I knew the only way to provide for my children was getting an education instead of only working and struggling to make my ends meet. I believed I could do things differently that would help me provide a better life for my sons. I moved to a nearby city and utilized the medical certification I earned before leaving my hometown to secure employment. My relationship with my close friends became strained, and the support I envisioned turned out to be a mirage, especially after Isaiah's murder. What I didn't know then, but know now, I was headed for some serious pitfalls that negatively impacted me and my sons.

Job 13:15 (ESV), "*Though he slay me, I will hope in Him; yet I will argue my ways to his face.*"

Job 13:15 was one aspect of the foundation I stood on. I was a single mom, and a damaged daughter, who surrounded herself with the wrong friends, and dated the wrong men because I didn't have the tools I needed to realize that I am intelligent, worthy, and loved. For seventeen years, God carried me through that and so much more. I learned how to lean on Him for everything. I built a stronger relationship with God through prayer, reading my Bible, and believing in what the Word of God told me. The one thing I desired, but did not have, is a connection to God's people, and they did not connect with my children either. They seemed so judgmental that I sought to protect myself by keeping myself isolated while burying myself in raising my children, providing them with a home, and working to support them. I was a faithful member of the Church and paid my tithes off of my meager salary of $26,000 per year. With my faithfulness to my Church, my relationship with God, and my actively saving money from each pay, I managed to save $7,000 to buy my first home.

Isaiah played school sports and participated in other outside activities, but his true love was dancing. He had swag, was cool as a cucumber, and we couldn't help but hype him up when he danced. Before YouTube was a thing, he produced a short video and uploaded it.

We attended and joined several churches while they were growing up, and now, looking back, I was pretty much ostracized and judged by the members and the leaders of those churches. It did not stop me from worshiping or going. What it did was stop me from believing and having an intimate relationship with Jesus Christ. I found myself straddling the fence instead of standing firm in my faith. Looking back, I realize my actions confused my children, while permitting me to continue allowing the wrong type of people in my life. I believed they supported me when in reality I was allowing the enemy to delay me from stepping fully into my purpose.

Although Isaiah was a bright light, he would get into trouble in school more often than not. I have to take responsibility for that, because I didn't know what I didn't know concerning the resources available to me, the various medications, and their side effects, and how to redirect his activities. Just as active as Isaiah was, he had a heart of gold. He would help the elderly with their groceries, raking their leaves, and/or taking out their trash. His big heart extended to the special relationship he had with his grandmother and his great-grandmother. Especially when his great-grandmother would share and break down the Bible stories they'd read together when he'd visit her and help with her care. After getting married, I had two more children that completed my family unit. Isaiah took his responsibility as a big brother to his two younger sisters, so seriously, we nick-named him "brother father." He used to laugh about how he tortured them about boys and their friends. He was an annoying, but jovial big brother who loved playing pranks and picking on his little sisters. We laughed at how he would tease the girls. That is until the day he was murdered!

I remember speaking with Isaiah the day before his death, and him telling me, "*Momma, you need to get out and have yourself some fun.*" I responded, "*You know what? You are right.*" I told him I would come to see him Sunday instead of Saturday, because I was going to go skating with a friend and her dance group to celebrate one of the ladies' birthday. At the time, we had a home and a condo. My husband and I spent most of our time at our home, while our adult children spent their time at the condo.

I was headed to my condo around 9:00 am when my husband told me I needed to charge my phone. First, let me be clear, I never let my phone die, and I always had my charger. Saturday night, the opposite happened. My phone died and I hadn't realized it! When I plugged my phone into the car charger, it started dinging and ringing! I couldn't respond since there were so many alarm bells and sirens going off all at once while I was driving. As I pulled into the condo's parking spot, I noticed I had missed calls and voicemail messages. The one that immediately caught my attention was from my Uncle Sam. Uncle Sam was a man of a few words who said what he meant and meant what he said. Before checking the missed calls and my other messages, I listened to Uncle Sam's voicemail message first. All he said was, "*Call your mamma.*"

Terrified and with shaky hands, I immediately scrolled, found, and tapped on my mother's name. While waiting for the phone to connect, I began thinking something was wrong with my grandmother. I surmised if something was wrong with her, Isaiah would be distraught even though she had been in a nursing home for the past two years. The phone rang once, and I said, "*Momma, did you call me? My phone was dead.*" She said, "*Call your brother.*" I responded, "*What is it, Mamma?*" I said it three or maybe four more times, "*what is it*"? All she would say was, "*Call your brother.*" Frustrated, I hung up with my mother, and called my little brother. When he answered, I said, "*Anthony, what is it? Momma said to call you.*" He said, "*It's Isaiah. He's dead!*" Incredulously, I said, "*What??? What do you mean?*" He replied, "*He's gone, Tom, He's gone.*" I bellowed out, "*No, no, no!, I can't! I have to go.*"

I immediately hung up and called my best friend. I was in denial! All I could think was my brother had lost his mind. There's no way that could be true. I had never questioned anything my brother had ever said to me, but this time my mind couldn't accept what he had said. I went straight into denial; I did not believe him. I couldn't, because the alternative was more than my heart could handle.

When my best friend answered, I asked, *"Do you know what happened last night? Did you hear anything about Isaiah?"* She answered, *"No."* I said, *"You don't know? You didn't hear anything?"* I told her what my brother said, and we both began to cry. I began to scream, and the next thing I knew, I had fallen out of my car onto the wet concrete, screaming. I'm not sure how long I was down there, but two angels came and scraped me off the wet ground and contacted my husband to come and get me.

Later, I received a call from the detective, and we set an appointment for me to pick up Isaiah's personal items: a watch, his house key, and his cell phone. Going forward, my life consisted of tears, tears, and more tears!!! This hurts so bad! I'm missing my son! My pain turned into anger. I was so damn mad at the murderer who took my son's life. I wanted revenge, and often thought of death. I wanted the coward who took my son's life to endure the same anguish and pain everyone who loved Isaiah experienced. I dreamt of going to his parents' house and asking them if they had something, they needed to say to me, seeing as though their son is the one who killed my son. It was so intense I could feel my eyes stinging and burning. My eyes itched whenever I closed them after the strain of hours of them being open. I was numb and couldn't feel a thing. I was a mess.

Even with everything going on, I had the presence of mind to pray. A good friend encouraged me to open my curtains and let the sunlight in to dismiss the darkness of grief that I was living with. It was a year, twelve full months before I remembered she spoke those words to me. I lost all sense of time and my good credit score. It felt like I was a hologram who moved and responded robotically. I cannot fully articulate the death that overtook my soul when my baby brother delivered the news that Sunday morning.

Isaiah was by no means perfect, but was a loving and respectable young man who enjoyed life. He didn't back down to anyone for any reason and proudly stood up for his family. He was a member of one of the largest families in our hometown. He was fun to be around and was the life of the party. His presence was missed at every event he failed to attend. To know him was to love and like him.

Isaiah loved the Lord, respected his elders, and honored women. He had a gentle spirit and would literally give you the shirt off his back. I am so grateful for that!

He would get into trouble as a youngster, and would say, '*the devil made me do it!*' Bless his little heart. I had to get on him and have my grandmother give him a good talking-to! One day, when Isaiah was about fifteen years old, he got himself into a situation that affected our whole family. When confronted, Isaiah apologized, and although I know he was sorry, I was still upset with him. As I was leaving out the house to take a walk on the Monon Trail by our condo, I remembered how he would say when he was younger, '*the devil made me do it!*'

I prayed for all my children regularly, but that morning I specifically prayed for Isaiah. God spoke to me and told me to "...*give him to Him; because it was finished.*" I didn't know exactly what that meant, but I said, "*Okay, God.*" As I began to walk faster, I looked up and Jared Scott Fogle, the Subway man, was walking in the opposite direction towards me. I was excited because he had lost all that weight, and I was going to speak or acknowledge him in some way. But as soon as we were shoulder to shoulder, I opened my mouth, and began speaking in other tongues as the Holy Spirit gave utterance. I could not believe it!

When I saw Isaiah for the first time after his spirit had left his body, I went into the mortuary and began to wail. I called on the name of Jesus and fell out. My cousins and my husband picked me up. I began to tarry, I called on God, I hollered, I screamed, I couldn't breathe, and I couldn't stand. I was weak, as if I hadn't eaten, slept, or drank for months. Which, now looking back on it, had been several weeks. As I began to call on the name of the Lord, He answered me. He said, "*I am with you, I have him. He is safe.*" When I heard that, I was slain in the spirit. I laid on the floor and cried out to God. My family let me stay there for who knows how long.

I'm not saying that to say, it took the pain away. I'm saying that because I knew what He meant when God said, "*It is finished.*" I met a beautiful mature woman at his home going. Her spirit was light and free, and her eyes were compassionate. I was blinded with sorrow, death, and emptiness, like none I had known before. But when she stood in front of me and held my hand, I felt something. Now that I have grown in my faith, I realize it was the Holy Spirit.

She told me he was such a friendly young man, and how he had helped her if he saw her out in her yard. He would tell her to rest, and he would do the chores for her. He also told her she did not need to pay him, and she said he shared his dreams with her whenever they spoke. It made my heart smile to know he touched others' lives in an impactful way. She looked forward to him stopping by to make sure she was alright.

I met so many wonderful people he loved and who loved him. One of the men from our neighborhood, Big John, my grandfather's buddy, and Isaiah played cards and listened to music together. During my conversation with some of them, they said he asked them how they felt about their salvation, and where they thought they would go if they died that night, heaven, or hell? That blew me away while knocking the wind out of me. The next morning, following his conversation with them, Isaiah was found lying face down from a gunshot wound to the back as he attempted to run away from a coward brandishing a gun. I cried myself to sleep last night in Mijyonna's bed, and woke up asking God, *"What is it that you require of me?"*

As I write Isaiah's story, tears fill my eyes. Two of those beautiful souls passed. Big John passed unexpectedly on July 10, 2019, from a car accident, and one month and a day after Isaiah died, his beloved great-grandmother passed. As I am sitting in the middle of a global pandemic, I realize God prepared me and so many others for such a time as this. I have to admit this pandemic isn't my first experience with devastation, isolation, and pain. For me, 2019 was a pandemic of the emotional kind.

God whispered to me consistently for eighteen months to get up. I couldn't gather the strength to move, and when I did, I was languid and weak. I felt like a dead woman walking. I couldn't love my other children or my grandchildren. I couldn't eat, I couldn't sleep, I didn't have conversations, I couldn't text, I couldn't type, I couldn't drive, and I rarely showered! I was, in all characteristics, dead. A piece of me died with my son. There were moments when I appeared present, but I don't recall anything discussed or mentioned, I was merely there.

It was from reading God's word, listening to spiritually healing music (the same Gospel music I played when my kids were young, and the same music Isaiah had on his playlist), and opening my curtains, allowing the sun to shine through that led me back to my heartland, God's light. I had died with Isaiah that summer, only to be born anew. God was moving and talking in, through, and for me.

It's been through God's word, my praise and worship sessions, and the interaction with my sisters and brothers in Christ (the relationships God has taken and the ones he has given) that I've grown spiritually. If not for the fasting, the praying, and the dreaming, I'd be an eating, drinking, and smoking zombie! The season of loss I went through taught me when someone experiences a loss, not to fix my mouth to speak on nor judge them. I now know the pain from loss firsthand.

"God blesses those who mourn, for they will be comforted." Matthew 5:4 (NLT) Three months before his murder, his great-grandmother told him she glimpsed him in heaven, and he was happy there. He smiled and said, *"Okay, grandma. I heard that."* They smiled and continued with their conversation. All I know is, Isaiah met her in heaven, one month and a day after he died.

My relationship with God was challenged. I was angry, bitter, jealous of mothers who still had their sons; and upset and disgusted that I had not thought of God while I was transitioning into being the mother of a murdered son. I felt like a fake. I know it wasn't anyone but the Holy Spirit who got me off my sofa, into the shower, and dressed. He even put my make-up on and drove my car to Heartland Church. When I got into the sanctuary, I cried out to God, *"Why? Why didn't You just leave my son alive? He had some struggles with addiction but was delivered from it. He was working on his GED and was doing wonderfully! He was positive, handsome, and walked by the name I gave him, Isaiah, the king Ali. We were all so proud of him."*

I know now this was God allowing Isaiah to get ready to come home. Isaiah's murderer turned himself in the same day he shot that murderous bullet. We as a family are now dealing with this devastating loss at the hands of a man that was someone Isaiah befriended. More often than not, this is true! Mothers of murdered children interact with their children's murderers and don't know it. Even today, mothers carry the pain of how their child's murderer could be one of their child's friends or associates. My prayers are for those individuals who selfishly took the lives of the many slain children to be brought to justice, and for the families of the slain to find peace.

Losing Isaiah thrust me into God's arms. I could not find peace in anything else I attempted to do. Whether it be drinking, having family and friends around me, or going places with my husband. I could not find peace. It wasn't until I started asking God to show me the way, and when I began to search God's word and study it, that I began to find the peace I had been searching for. I learned how to lean on His promises, trust in His Word, the importance of meditation, the necessity of fasting, and the healing powers of prayer. I craved interaction with other believers and was active in Kingdom work. When my son was murdered, it felt like my soul had died, but during my grief, God was rejuvenating my Spirit. God started sending me angels, one by one. They poured into me, and they prayed for me. I researched and joined support groups and took my daughters and Isaiah's son to grief counseling. I am not saying these steps were simple and easy to do. What I am saying is it was necessary. While grieving Isaiah's loss, I also was grieving the loss of lifelong friends. Friends I had loved and who loved me back vanished! They were gone! Some without warning, others after blow-ups, leaving me to grieve their loss while struggling to accept and grieve Isaiah's loss.

I had a mental breakdown. I was in a valley of depression and felt like I had lost my mind. I asked my doctor for medication to help me sleep, and was told no! I couldn't believe she told me no! That's when I told her to write it in my medical records, she asked why? I replied, "*you denied me care. I want to go walk in front of a bus because I have not slept in months.*" She then told me, "*Well, you need to go see a therapist.*" I said, "*I see a therapist bi-weekly in this same building.*" She then said, "*Then the therapist should write you a prescription.*" I replied, "*You're my PMP! Why can't you help me?*" She said, "*Because that medicine is addictive,*" and I said, "*I do not have a history of addiction for myself, nor is there a history of addiction in my bloodline. Just make sure you write that in my medical records.*"

Not only was I grieving my son, but I was being treated like a second-class citizen when receiving adequate mental health care. I was severely depressed. I could not focus, when I tried to do the things I loved, like cooking, it never turned out right. My credit score dropped, I did not have the energy to open my mail, nor did I even think about it. I was failing in my professional life, and the company that employed me worked with me as much as they could. My debilitating grief caused me not to be successful, because I was unable to focus on my projects, causing them to be doomed to fail.

Isaiah's loss had such a detrimental effect on my mental health, it caused me to experience severe setbacks emotionally and mentally. I know it wasn't 'anything but the blood of Jesus' that brought me out. Isaiah's loss caused me to reevaluate my life, my relationships, and my mental health. Today, I can take nature walks, and bask in the bright sunshine shining on my face as I remember my son. The journey of loss and my battle with mental illness inspired me to create a nonprofit organization, "What Elephant, Inc.," to help survivors and families of gun violence in honor of my son.

We miss you so much, Isaiah Dakeem ♥, I'm coming back up son. ♥ ♥ ♥ Your loss muffled me, but God has given me my voice back. He's given me strength and angels to endure these last 554 days without you. Love you later!

Thank you to all those who have been praying for us.

In Loving Memory:
Isaiah Dakeem Ali Horton

JOURNAL PROMPT

If one day you received "the call" how do you think you would respond?

If you could say just one thing to one of your children that you think they already know, what would it be?

_____

_____

_____

_____

_____

_____

_____

_____

_____

_____

_____

_____

_____

_____

_____

_____

Photo Credit: Color Craft

CHAPTER 8: Author - Wendy McIntosh

Wendy McIntosh was born and raised in Indianapolis, Indiana and has been married for eighteen years. She is the mother of three children, two boys and one girl. She is currently working in women's health as a Medical Assistant. She has over twenty years of experience in the healthcare industry. Wendy achieved her MA Certification in 2007 and has not turned back. Wendy has also enrolled in Nursing School and is taking a leap of faith to becoming an infamous author. Wendy has been blessed to have had the opportunity to work in multiple roles in Healthcare. She has worked in Hospice as a Volunteer Service Coordinator/Hospice Aide, and with a traveling physician company as a Patient Care Coordinator/MA and Home Healthcare as an HHA. Working in Hospice was a rewarding experience that has allowed her to service and help many families throughout

Indiana. The knowledge and experience that she gained through bereavement and grief has helped her in her own journey. Wendy has carried out several speaking engagements for multiple healthcare events, raising awareness and discussing the importance of patient support and patient advocacy, and coordinated health fairs. This encouraged Wendy to start and manage her own events company "Unforgettable Times" where she manages events such as weddings and other celebrations.

Wendy's most celebrated accomplishment was raising her children and encouraging them that "they can do anything that they set their minds to". She and her husband are hoping to relocate and take an early retirement. When she is not studying or writing, you can find Wendy on the beach singing, dancing, decorating or working on new arts/crafts.

CHAPTER 8: THERE'S A SON BEYOND THE CLOUDS

"Trust in the Lord with all thine heart; and lean not unto thine own understanding."
-Proverbs 3:5

I was nineteen years old when I found out I was pregnant with my eldest son. I was afraid and unprepared. I didn't know what to do, or which way to go. Although I had friends who were pregnant between the ages of fourteen and sixteen years old, I was still embarrassed, ashamed, and hesitant to tell my mom. Several weeks passed, and I finally got the courage to tell my mom, and the expression on her face showed her disappointment in me.

During my pregnancy, I became sick, weak, and unable to keep food down. I often went to the Emergency Room (ER) due to my throat being inflamed from consistent vomiting. This caused me to lose weight and experience depression. My OBGYN Physician decided to do extensive lab testing. From the tests, I found out I had a rare blood type that required monitoring during my pregnancy. I was referred to a Maternal-Fetal Medicine Specialist for further testing. There was some confusion with my gestational age, even after an extensive ultrasound was performed, which led them to believe my baby wasn't developing properly. During the appointment, the doctor informed me my child could have Down Syndrome or other complications. They recommended I take an Amniocentesis test that required a needle to be placed into my placenta and fluid drawn. This test can cause a high risk for miscarriages. I could not understand how this was happening to me when I never drank or smoked in my life. I did not have the support from my son's father, who had his own struggles and health issues. Fearing judgment from his family, he became overwhelmed and confused, and started having behavioral issues. None of which were healthy for me or my pregnancy. So, we decided it was best he kept his distance. It wasn't until a year later I found out he'd been murdered, and to my shock and horror, his body went unidentified during that whole time.

I had to make some important decisions, but I couldn't do it on my own. This forced me to seek my mother's help to make the right choices. My mother realized how sick I was, and decided to accept the fact that I was pregnant, and became supportive and encouraging. My mom told me to start praying more and trust in God. She also told me my baby would be okay, and said she disagreed with the doctors' diagnosis. She then emphatically said, *"God has the final say."* I started receiving mail from *Mothers with Down Syndrome* children support groups as if I accepted it as my son's story. It was then I took my mother's advice. I refused to allow anything else to put a strain on me and my unborn child. I did everything within my power to have a healthy baby, and to give my son every opportunity in life. I declined the Amniocentesis test, and other genetic tests and counseling! I refused to take the risk.

At 9:30 am on June 17, 2000, I gave birth to a healthy baby boy. He weighed in at 6 lbs., 9 oz, and was 19 inches long. He had all ten of his fingers and toes. I remember telling the doctor, *"…let me see my son,"* before they cleaned him up. I looked into my son's eyes and said, "*Welcome son!*" He was the most beautiful baby I had ever seen, with chocolate skin and dark, soft, and smooth hair. Right then and there, I committed to loving and protecting him, regardless of what anyone said. Even though the doctor had to wiggle him to make him cry, there were no signs of Down Syndrome or any other health issues. Not long after Rayshawn's birth, I got my first tattoo on my left shoulder. The tattoo is of a boy angel with wings holding on to a ribbon with my son's name, Rayshawn, on it. I believed he was an angel sent to me by God to help me understand the meaning of love, and was a symbol to remind me that my struggles were worth it.

I was not alone while raising Rayshawn, because a wonderful man came into my life, who became Rayshawn's father and my husband. We became a blended family. Rayshawn was an energetic baby and started crawling around six months and walking around tables at nine months. However, he was afraid to step out on his own and refused to walk unaccompanied until he was thirteen and a half months. As you can imagine, he was spoiled and discriminatory with whom he would allow to hold him. He learned a lot from his step-siblings, and I watched him grow into a curious toddler. As a family tradition, Rayshawn was given the nickname Ray-Ray by his grandmother. On his third birthday, Rayshawn said he received the best birthday present in the world. I had another baby born three years to the day of his birthday, on June 17, 2003. He told everyone he wasn't going to have a birthday party because he had already gotten the best gift ever, a baby brother. He was the best big brother anyone could ever ask for. He took his job seriously and would always watch over his brother. He felt responsible for him and was attentive to his needs. He played with him and gathered his diapers and wipes throughout the day. When he started pre-school, he was grieved at leaving his brother, while being excited and ready to start school. It meant the world to him to ride the school bus for the first time. I explained to him he'd have to ride it alone. When the school bus picked him up, he asked me to come and sit next to him. After a while, he was okay with riding by himself. He couldn't wait to get home and tell me all about his day.

Rayshawn welcomed a baby sister on January 6, 2005. He was overjoyed, but couldn't understand why she wasn't born on his birthday. I explained to him several times that all babies are not born on his birthday. When he came to the hospital to visit his sister for the first time. He asked, how long will it be before my birthday comes? I told him she's his early birthday gift from God. He showed his sister so much love and was attentive to her needs. He was my little helper. I have always said Rayshawn was beyond his years. He would say things that would startle everyone. He said to me, "*next time have another boy because girls cry too much.*" I told him his mom is not planning to have another baby unless it's God's will. The expression on his face was one of relief. What most people did not know about Rayshawn was he was terrified of bugs and insects. I remember one Christmas we purchased fake insects and placed them around the Christmas tree to keep him from sneaking into the presents. As the story was shared with my husband's family, they affectionately nicknamed him 'chicken.'

I will never forget the time when Rayshawn begged me to allow him to spend a night at his Auntie's house, so he could play with his cousins. Rayshawn was seven years old at the time. My sister decided to take Rayshawn and her children to the park. I had just gotten off work and was in the process of eating dinner with my two youngest children. I received a call from my sister telling me my son was injured and to meet her at the ER. My sister stated Rayshawn was on the Merry-Go-Round, holding on to the bar when my niece started spinning it around. His hands slipped off the handlebars, and he landed on his left shoulder and popped his left collar bone out of place. Once I arrived, I saw my son sitting in a wheelchair in severe pain, with a brace around his neck and two straps across his body. My son could not cry or verbalize words due to the pain. I immediately wrapped my arms around my son and held him. I screamed at the hospital staff and asked them, "*Why is my baby still sitting out here?*" There was a patient in the waiting area who witnessed my outburst and generously requested they take Rayshawn in their place. They gave him pain medications and sedated him. Two surgeons came in to try and push his bone back into place. Rayshawn felt the pain from their manipulation of his arm, the sedation didn't work. Things went from bad to worse as Rayshawn fought with the surgeons and jerked with every manipulation they performed during the procedure. I couldn't watch them hurt my son any longer, and had to step outside the room, so they could successfully help him. He was released in an arm sling, and I had to gently care for and monitor him. As time went on, you could barely notice he had the injury. He played sports like any other kid.

It brought me such joy to watch him as he grew into an amazingly caring young man. I would always get compliments on how respectful and considerate he was. We could be at a restaurant, church, visiting, or in school, and people always came up to me and said positive things about Rayshawn. This made me happy to know he was an excellent reflection of our family teachings. His great attitude and intelligence brought him so many awards and recognitions throughout his education. He led his sixth-grade graduation ceremony, gave a speech, and helped with the program. He received six awards that day, and I felt so proud watching him shine. He continued to take his education seriously and attended math and science camp during the summer.

Things changed during his high school years, it started to become a challenge to him. Rayshawn struggled with communicating his feelings and the things going on with him. My husband and I noticed the changes in him and decided to have him see a therapist to help him develop the tools and build the confidence to communicate the changes he was experiencing mentally, emotionally, and physically. Although he continued getting good grades, he struggled with trying to find his place in the world. He had a lot of pressure on him during this time, but still managed to have a positive attitude. He was chosen to be in the Upward Bound Program. In this program, he had to maintain passing grades, at least a 2.5 grade point average, and have a willingness to learn. This program offered him the opportunity to experience college life at the IUPUI campus, the ability to take college courses while in high school, and a scholarship to attend college. Rayshawn traveled out of town for educational tours and assisted with different community activities throughout Indianapolis, Indiana, as a part of the program. His dream was to become a pharmacist and a part-time chef. I encouraged him to go after his dreams, especially since he was good at math and science. My favorite quote I would tell him all the time was, "*The sky is the limit!*" It encouraged and empowered Rayshawn to start figuring out his plans towards adulthood.

Rayshawn meant the world to me, and he was the catalyst in me growing up and becoming an adult. He helped me realize there's life beyond my expectations. What I thought was going to be a struggle turned out to be one of my greatest blessings. Being his mother gave me a new appreciation of motherhood. Rayshawn's life was taken away from us on April 22, 2020, two months before his twentieth birthday. For a period of time, Rayshawn was involved in a social media beef with another young man, where the young man felt Rayshawn had disrespected him. During one of their encounters, Rayshawn and the young man fought. However, in the young man's eyes, the issue was not resolved. Their last encounter happened on April 22, 2020, when they met to work through their disagreement, but the other young man had murder on his mind and gunned Rayshawn down in cold blood. I was called to the scene to identify my son's body that day. I was praying this was not true. I cried until I was numb, and my tears were all dried up. So many thoughts went through my head, but the one that haunted me was '...did he call out for me.' Words could not express my pain nor my thoughts of him lying on the ground lifeless. If I had to put it into words, I would say, "*It felt like an elephant was sitting on my chest and I couldn't move.*" My grief was painful. I was in agony while experiencing body aches and headaches. This cannot be happening! I was in disbelief. Even to this day, it feels like I am in a nightmare, one I cannot wake up from. I had so many hopes and dreams for my son that will never be fulfilled. Knowing I will never see my son or hear his laugh again is the hardest part of it all for me. I am in constant contact with the detectives assigned to Rayshawn's case. The case will be going to trial soon, and I pray daily there will be justice for Rayshawn.

Under no circumstances should a mother have to bury a child. It affects an entire family and community. This left us with an empty hole in our hearts, and there will always be a void. Some say God doesn't make mistakes. I disagree, because I feel like this is not an act of God. To create a human being for a mother to pour her heart into and nurture, and then to purposely take the child away, makes me question, why? This has caused me to rebuild my relationship with God. I may never understand the loss of my son, but I know that God is keeping me and my family as we grieve Rayshawn's life, death, and unrealized hopes and dreams. I do not want to ever justify, or make an excuse for, the pain my family and I have endured. Rayshawn's younger sister and brother are the main reason I haven't fallen into depression or given up. They are the ones who motivate me to wake up and keep going. Watching their strength encourages me daily. God blessed me to birth other children. I cannot be selfish, and I will not give up on them. I am learning how to cope and deal with this ongoing pain. The two things I can confirm, and I've learned throughout this unfortunate journey, are: "I'm much stronger than I've ever known," and "I view life's challenges differently, now." Rayshawn left us to cherish so many memories, and he will always be in our hearts. The one thing that gives me peace and makes my heart smile whenever I think of Rayshawn is "to know, him was to love him."

The grief my family and I are dealing with has forced us to realize we cannot take this journey alone. Since Rayshawn's death, my Church family has been there supporting us and has given us the opportunity to share our memories of him in a healthy way. Through counseling, we are learning how to cope with his murder and the great loss we feel.

All this led to me joining the support group *'Purpose for My Pain.'* The openness of the group, our conversations and their support have and is helping me take this journey as I realize I am not alone.

John 16:33
"These things I have spoken unto you, that in me ye might have peace. In the world ye shall have tribulation: but be of good cheer; I have overcome the world."

In Loving Memory:
Rayshawn Delany McIntosh

JOURNAL PROMPT

How have you been able to rely on your faith to overcome the obstacles you've experienced while raising your child(ren) and/or during your season of grief? When experiencing your loss, what ways have you questioned God or wondered if He was right there with you?

_____

_____

_____

_____

_____

_____

_____

_____

_____

_____

_____

_____

_____

_____

_____

_____

Photo Credit – Tavis Wallace with Taj Images and Photography

CHAPTER 9: Author - Tisa Whack

Tisa Whack was born in Charleston, South Carolina and is the daughter of Mr. Blease Whack and the late Cheryl Whack-Stevenson. She is the oldest of three girls, the mother of one son, the late Tyrell, the grandmother of one grandson De'ion, and mother-in-law to Tiffany.

Tisa has been employed with MUSC Physicians for twenty-five years where she started as a file clerk and has held varies roles with the most current role as a Patient Account Manager. Tisa's work ethic and passion for people within Health Administration has deemed her an asset to MUSC Health and has ranked as a Tier 1 Leader within the organization. Tisa believes in leading her team by drawing out their capabilities, providing them the tools they need to be successful and grow within the organization.

Tisa holds a bachelor's degree in business administration with a concentration in Management and is currently pursuing her master's degree in business management with a concentration in Project Management.

Tisa is the co-founder of the nonprofit organization *"We Are Their Voices"*. This organization was birthed in 2017 after the tragic loss of her son and only child due to senseless gun violence. Through this organization, Tisa works to create awareness and communication among young adults and communities regarding the impact of gun violence. The organization is the "voice" of gun violence victims who can no longer speak for themselves and provides access, outlets, and opportunities to help troubled young men divert from negativity and gun violence. They also host monthly support meetings for families.

Tisa is also a founding member of *Taking Back Our Village*, an advisory board established in 2014 that consist of community members, volunteers, and law enforcement within Charleston County Sheriff's Office who are dedicated to improving the overall well-being of our local communities. They promote activities that will empower citizens, strengthen families, and encourage young people to become productive members of society.

In addition, Tisa is an active member of *Everytown for Gun Safety, Moms Demand Action for Gun Sense in America* - Charleston Chapter Community Lead, Deputy Chapter Lead for SC Chapter of *Moms Demand Action*, and a Survivor Fellow with *Everytown Survivor Network*.

Tisa is committed to being Tyrell's voice as she brings awareness to the impact of gun violence.

CHAPTER 9: THE UNFORESEEN MILESTONES

By

Tisa Whack

"Tyrell's amazing smile, heart, and personality will always be cherished and live within his son."
-Tisa Whack

God was preparing me for what the enemy believed would destroy me. The preparation did not appear at the time, and as I was constantly being told, my weeping may endure for the night but joy cometh in the morning. I keep asking what morning... I am reminded God does not operate in time as I do, nor by watching the minutes, the hours, and the days go by.

As I think about what I want the world to know, how I turned my unimaginable pain and suffering into purpose, and how I honor my one and only child Tyrell; I am reminded of circumstances around his birth, his life, and his death. Tyrell arrived in this world via emergency C-section because his heart rate dropped every time, I had a contraction. His extraordinary story doesn't end there! At the age of 5, he almost drowned, at the age of 17 he almost died in a major motor vehicle accident (MVA) that resulted in a traumatic brain injury (TBI) and the death of another, at the age of 19 he diagnosed with grand mal seizures (one time I found him motionless on the bathroom floor near death), and finally at the age of 23 murdered by gun violence.

You see, I dreamt his death exactly the way it happened the year before... I felt it in my soul, was God preparing me? Did his death birth my purpose? Allow me to share my journey as a mother who lost her only child and became a survivor, an advocate, and a mentor through it all.

At the age of 19, I gave birth to Tyrell via emergency C-section. His original due date was September 7, 1992, but he arrived two weeks early. No manual accompanied him at birth, I only had my instincts and what I learned from my mother to guide me. It was me and him against the world, and I was determined to take care of him and protect him from the world.

Tyrell was a fighter! His fight began before birth and continued for 23 years. It was as if from birth the enemy knew greatness was within him and did not want it to come to fruition. As his mother, I was constantly in protection mode, which was sometimes problematic since he was an extremely independent, and fearless, kid who trusted without a second thought. I recall at the age of five I signed him up for little league baseball and after an impressive season, we were invited to the end of the season party at one of his teammate's parents' home. They had a pool and Tyrell was so excited, even though he did not know how to swim yet. We stopped at the local Wal-Mart on the way there to get swim floaties since I knew he could not swim. Once we arrived and parked, other parents arrived simultaneously. Tyrell and the other boys from the team raced towards the house ahead of us heading straight for the backyard and, yes, you guessed it, the swimming pool. Before I knew it, I had lost sight of him, and before I could get to the backyard he had headed to the slide and made his way into the pool. By the time I got to the pool, he was completely under and was not coming up. I could not swim so a parent jumped in and got him out.

As he was laying on the side of the pool, he looked gray in the face and was given CPR, and he immediately started coughing and opened his eyes. The terror on his face had me in tears, but God saved him and within about an hour he eventually eased back into the pool but with my guarded eyes on him. I was so nervous but did not want to discourage him from going back into the water. We ended that day with a scare and learned some invaluable lessons: 1. Teach your kid to swim early and 2. My son is a fighter.

Tyrell and I continued to learn lessons after lessons together as we navigated the world. At the time, he was the only boy in our family as we were a family of females. His dad stayed about four hours away, so he mainly visited him during the summer months, Christmas break, and long holiday weekends. He loved his time with his dad while exploring his dad's hometown of Dillon, SC, and visiting with his two brothers. This routine went on for years until Tyrell was in 8th grade when his father's truck driving job became more demanding. As his dad spent most of his time on the road driving, Tyrell's interest in spending the entire summer in Dillon away from his friends diminished.

Tyrell's close-knit group of friends consisted of his cousin and a few neighborhood friends. They were all one year older than Tyrell, but he hung in there with them. Normal pre-teen and teenage boy activities like community football, basketball, and baseball leagues led to high school football for Tyrell. Like every parent in America, I dealt with the teenage dirty room, late-night video gaming, and hanging out with his friends playing basketball every chance they could. I must say life with a teenage boy was calm for me. Life was simple for us and as a single parent, I worked diligently to lead by example.

In 2009, Tyrell's everyday friends graduated from high school and moved on to college. I remember talking with him saying, *"Tyrell, who will you hang out with now? All your friends have gone to college."* He simply stated, "*I'm good, Ma.*" You see Tyrell had a wonderful personality and did not have trouble meeting new people. He had other friends he'd met along the way who were not his day-to-day friends. In the back of my mind, I worried just a little because he could be so trusting of everyone and I knew his friends who graduated were true friends in his life.

Now Tyrell is a high school senior, class of 2010. My son and only child is about to graduate and will be heading off to college soon. School starts in August for us, and Tyrell recently celebrated his 17th birthday on the 21st. He started hanging out with friends he already knew but was not around regularly before this school year. Little did I know less than 30 days later our lives and the lives of others would change dramatically. Against my better judgment, I let Tyrell attend his high school's football game. It was an important rival game in our area, and he begged me to go even though he got in trouble at school earlier that week for cutting class. I told him to be home by midnight no later. I woke up about 12:30 am to discover he was not home yet and started calling his cell phone, but no answer. It was going directly to voicemail. He was known to never keep that phone charged. I called repeatedly! I was getting angry because he missed curfew. I was kicking myself for letting him go in the first place. At this point, I started calling his friends to see if they knew where he was but got no answer. It is now 2 am and still no Tyrell! I am now pacing the floor and getting madder by the moment. Then the phone rings, it's my mom. She tells me the police are at her door, and Tyrell was in a car accident. Tyrell was transported to the Medical University of South Carolina (MUSC). My mom lived across town, and since I hadn't changed my vehicle registration, they went to her house. I did not have a car to get to the hospital and it was about 20-30 minutes away from my apartment. I called my twin sister who lived nearby, and we headed to the hospital. I honestly did not know what to expect. I learned from the officer who went to my mom's house, the accident happened less than ten minutes from our apartment, but they transported him to a trauma hospital. I anticipated the worst. The drive to the hospital was the longest ever. I called his father in route to let him know what was going on. He was hours away on the road in Virginia. I would just have to call him and fill him in as soon as I found out more. We finally arrived at the hospital and gave the front desk Tyrell's name. They didn't have any information. They couldn't find him in the system, and I almost lost it. No one could tell us anything. They told us to wait, and they'd try to find something out. We stepped outside and moments later a man approached us and asked if we were Tyrell's family. I said yes, and when I finally focused on the speaker, I noticed the word CHAPLIN on his badge. I immediately started backing away from him and started crying harder. All I could think of was this man was here to tell me Tyrell died. I needed to get away from him, but my knees gave out and I found myself on the ground crying. He realized his appearance upset me and immediately told me Tyrell's not dead. He's in critical condition. When I read his badge, I assumed the worst, and he had no idea. When the doctor came out to speak with us, he stated Tyrell was in a head-on collision and suffered serious trauma. Both ankles were broken, his left tibia was fractured, his right femur was broken, and he had a head injury to which they did not know the extent of, yet. Wow... was all I could think as I listened to the doctor with my sisters by my side. My family had arrived and were listening as the doctor told me about Tyrell's condition.

As we're outside, the highway patrol officers arrived and explained Tyrell was in a head-on collision accident where he somehow crossed the center line and hit another car. Unfortunately, the person in the other car did not survive. My heart sank... All I could think was 'What in the hell happened? Oh, my God, someone died!'

As the night passed, the doctors told us Tyrell was in the ICU and the next few hours would be critical. He suffered a Traumatic Brain Injury (TBI) to the frontal lobe, and they couldn't tell the extent of the injury. They needed to allow his body to rest. The swelling in his brain needed to come down. It was a waiting game. They weren't able to address the other injuries until they could stabilize him. My son laid still in a hospital bed unresponsive as another family received life-shattering news of the loss of their loved one.

As the news of Tyrell's accident spread, my family and friends started showing up at the hospital. It got crowded because I have a huge family, especially on my father's side. They literally lined the entire hallway outside of the ICU waiting room as we held hands and prayed for Tyrell's recovery, and the other impacted family. While grasping all that had occurred, a thought popped into my head... 'I was scheduled to close on my first home in a matter of days. What am I doing thinking about closing on my first home in a couple of days when my son is in the hospital, in critical condition and there's no idea if he will survive! To even make the situation worse there's a family mourning the loss of their loved one as a result of the accident Tyrell caused. Come on, Tisa, get it together!' All I could do was pray God would help Tyrell pull through this tragedy.

A few days later my real estate agent called saying we're scheduled to close on my house the same day Tyrell's trauma team told me he's scheduled for surgery with the orthopedic surgeon. If you've ever purchased a house, you know you might not know the exact closing costs until the day before or even at the last minute. My mind was all over the place! I had doctors to contend with, family coming in and out asking for updates, and to top it off I am being asked by my agent and builder if I wanted to reschedule due to the circumstances. I told them, no, I would proceed with the closing as planned. Most would ask why not reschedule, but I had conversations with God as I struggled between doing the closing and being at the hospital with Tyrell. God told me to proceed with the closing as He planned for me and to trust Him to take care of Tyrell. I tapped into my faith, listened to God's voice, and followed His direction. By doing so, I felt at peace with my decision.

My mom and sisters remained at the hospital while Tyrell was in surgery to repair the multiple injuries to both legs. I closed on the house, got the keys, left the lawyer's office, and headed quickly back to the hospital to learn the surgery was a success. One prayer had been answered in a big way, I had the keys to my dream home! God promised to take care of Tyrell, and I was standing on that promise in anticipation of Tyrell recuperating in our new home.

Tyrell remained in the Surgical Trauma Intensive Care Unit, and daily I watched the doctors, and their residents discuss his case every morning during rounds. His condition remained uncertain, and they told me daily it's a wait-and-see game. To watch my child in that hospital bed and not able to do anything but wait was heart-wrenching and stressful. I found myself trying to navigate what I should and should not be doing. Which in and of itself was tough. Yet I found myself monitoring Tyrell's friends to determine which were coming out of concern and who was being nosy, only coming to take pictures of him to post on social media. It got to the point where I requested only those on the list, I provided, could visit Tyrell. I needed to ensure there was as much positive energy around my son as I prayed for him, the healing from his injuries and his recuperation. As one week turned into two. I visited Tyrell with all the machines monitoring his vitals, and to my dismay, a tracheotomy and a feeding tube were installed. During the daily update on Tyrell's condition, his medical team said they tried to ween him off the medications, keeping him sedated, but his body was not ready to work on its own yet. I honestly did not know what else to do but continue praying.

Tyrell's paternal grandfather, Charles, and maternal grandmother, Cheryl, camped out at the hospital in a quiet waiting room area many did not know about. They spent their days waiting and taking turns sitting with Tyrell in his ICU room. They talked with him and prayed he could hear them. Tyrell's father, DeAnzio, finally arrived in town.

He sat with Tyrell. Tyrell is the youngest of his three sons. He shared with me how helpless he felt because there was nothing, he could do to make Tyrell better. Tyrell's girlfriend, Tiffany, came daily to check on him not knowing if she would ever talk to him again. I was traveling back and forth between the hospital and moving since my lease was up. I needed to move everything to my new home across town. After my sisters and I packed everything up, my boyfriend, Clayton, moved everything to the new house for me. I was supposed to be excited about the new house, but I couldn't! My son was in the ICU and there wasn't any guarantee he'd ever make it out of the hospital alive. I spent the next five weeks going back and forth to the hospital, staying until visitation hours ended for the ICU unit, going home to cry and attempt to get some rest. As people visited the hospital, they'd often ask how I can be so calm. I guess they expected me to fall apart every time they saw me. It was not that I was such a strong person, it was my complete reliance on my faith that God would bring my son through. My faith is where my calm and peace came from. If I am being honest, it was the only thing keeping me together.

By God's grace, Tyrell recovered from the accident and was released to a rehab facility for a complete recovery. When released from the rehab center, although in a wheelchair, he came home to our new house and his new room. Tyrell was a huge North Carolina Tarheels Basketball fan, and to his surprise, a close family friend had painted the logo on his bedroom wall. Tyrell had to be carried upstairs since he was unable to walk. Tyrell's return home was a blessing pitted with challenges. He had daily physical therapy appointments due to the injuries to his ankles and legs, and I noticed issues with Tyrell's short-term memory, judgment making, and temperament due to his TBI, which also affected his cognitive development. He was homeschooled, so he could graduate with his class. After a while, Tyrell transferred to e-learning and received his diploma.

A year after Tyrell's accident and recovery he had a grand mal seizure while at my mom's house which put him in the hospital, the same hospital he was sent to when he had the accident. They intubated Tyrell, and we were in another scary situation not knowing if Tyrell would wake up from the trauma of the seizure. He eventually awoke and the doctors told us Tyrell has epilepsy, and they're unsure if it's what caused the previous year's accident or a result of the accident. The stress of it all seemed as if we were living in a never-ending nightmare. At this point, I'm mentally exhausted and wondering why my son must suffer through so much. I questioned what I had done wrong as a parent that might be causing so much trauma in my son's life. Was there something from my past exacting a price from him? At 18, Tyrell went through so much, and I did not know how to fix any of it. He went to therapy to talk about the accident, his current health issues, and the life laid out before him. Tyrell had no memory of the accident, and since no one was in the car with him, there was no one to fill in the gaps in his memory. I believed Tyrell struggled with what happened but didn't know how to express himself. After a few visits, with a therapist, he did not want to continue, so I did not force him. He was old enough to decide and I did not want to press the issue. I prayed with him and for him, and we leaned on our church family and pastor for guidance, strength, and support.

We had several more critical hospital moments due to Tyrell's epilepsy. He took some of the highest doses of medication to keep his epilepsy under control. It was hard for him to remember to take it. He was a young adult and the last thing on his mind was taking medication. We managed the best we could under the circumstances. Tyrell's girlfriend spent several days in the hospital with him and attempted to encourage him. They met in high school and were still together through all his tragedies. Some would have expected her to have jumped ship a long time ago, but not Tiffany. She's been there for Tyrell through it all, and he needed her to balance him out because he was having a rough time. As he navigated living with epilepsy and being a young adult, we had our ups and downs. He did not always agree with the advice I offered and would often get himself caught up in more trouble than it was worth.

As life started to level off for Tyrell, in 2012, Clayton and I went out for a movie and dinner. I was not feeling well all week. I was experiencing some awful heartburn, but I made the best of it and enjoyed the night out. Still feeling horrible the next morning, I went to an urgent care facility to get checked out. They performed some tests and eventually referred me to the same hospital Tyrell had been admitted to for additional tests. I was confused and kept pondering why they were sending me here for heartburn. Several tests later, they told me I had cancer, Non-Hodgkin Lymphoma. The ride from the doctor's office back home was a blur. I was in shock. I had cancer! Within a week, I was going back and forth to the doctor to prepare for chemo and my first day of treatment accompanied by Clayton, Tyrell, and my twin sister, Tanisha. I spent the next six months in treatment and wondering will life ever calm down. While in prayer, I asked God to heal my body. I worked as much as I could, during the process. During those six months of treatment, Tyrell came to me and said he had something to tell me. He informed me, he and Tiffany were having a baby and the baby was due in December 2012. I must admit I was a little upset with him because he was not ready for such a responsibility. He needed a stable job, and he needed to get his life on track before taking on such a huge responsibility.

At this point, Tyrell had encounters with law enforcement and was on probation. The accident affected his judgment-making abilities which created challenges with him finding employment. I was helping him financially and through prayer, in helping him get his life together and being a great dad. I finished my last chemo treatment on October 2, 2012, two weeks before my fortieth birthday, and welcomed my grandson into the world on December 4, 2012. I fell in love with him the moment I laid eyes on him. It was one of the greatest experiences in my life, welcoming my first grandchild into the world.

The next year was a challenge for Tyrell, his epilepsy got progressively worse. He spent a significant amount of time going back and forth to the hospital for care and for increases in his daily medication regimen. He experienced fluctuations in his weight as the doctors tried to find the right course of medication to control his epilepsy. Daily, I feared what his epilepsy and the side effects of the drugs were doing to Tyrell. On top of that, Tyrell struggled with making wise choices due to the TBI. He was arrested with a group of young adults for breaking and entering because he was with them, and not because he participated in the crime. During his time in jail, Tyrell was having seizures, but there wasn't anything I could do for him while he was there. One night I remember waking up screaming from a horrible nightmare. I dreamt Tyrell was shot and killed while sitting in the front seat of a car. In the dream, my niece called to tell me what happened. My screams, during the dream, caused Clayton to wake up and ask me what was wrong. The dream was so vivid and real, it scared the hell out of me. I never told anyone else about the dream except Clayton.

The attorney I hired sought probation for Tyrell instead of taking the case to trial and him possibly having to spend five years in prison. Even now, I wonder if that was the best course of action for him. As a mother, I felt I had failed in protecting my son. Years later, we are still observing the effects of the accident.

In Dec 2014, my mom was rushed to the hospital. After admitting her to the hospital, she was rushed into surgery to have a pacemaker installed. During her recovery, I visited her on Christmas Day and went home to get some much-needed rest. Before her admittance to the hospital, Mom had been on dialysis for years, and when we went to visit her the next day, she was unable to speak. She lapsed into a diabetic coma because her blood sugar had dropped to 27. My sisters and I were devastated and did not know what to do. The hospital didn't have an explanation except to tell us she may never wake up and if she did, they could not guarantee what her quality of life would look like. Decisions had to be made concerning Mom's care that forced my twin sister, Tanisha, and my baby sister, Nakia, and I to come together and make them. On January 14, 2015, Mom passed away, one day before her 62nd birthday. The rock of our family was gone, without us ever receiving answers to what caused Mom's rapid decline. This was not only a monumental blow for the family but a blow for Tyrell, as well. I remember Tyrell crying, like a baby, at her funeral. He was her first grandchild, and they shared a strong bond.

An already difficult life became even harder as we struggled to learn how to navigate life without our mom. The shock of her death was still fresh as we attempted to wrap our hearts around what our heads knew was our truth. During this time, Tyrell and Tiffany moved back home to save money to get their own place. Tyrell found work through temporary services, but he longed for something more stable and permanent. Tyrell would spend most of his time with Tiffany and his son. He loved him so dearly and Tiffany did not have to lift a finger when it came to their son. Tiffany and Tyrell started attending Church together. They both belonged to a Church before they met. Although he was active in his church, he longed to join Tiffany at the church she attended, and his uncle pastored. In July 2015, Tyrell and Tiffany got married and Tyrell was baptized the following September. I still remember Tyrell strolling in the kitchen one day and during a conversation with him, I said to myself 'My Tyrell is back!' You see this was the first time since the accident it seemed Tyrell was himself. It made my heart smile! Later, I invited him to watch me complete a half-marathon on November 12, 2015. I participated in half-marathons once I completed the cancer treatments to help me stay motivated and healthy. This was the first time Tyrell watched me run and finish the marathon. I don't know which of us was more excited. He came with his wife, Tiffany, and my grandson. At the end of the

Marathon, we took pictures and Tyrell said he'd be there for my next race in December to cheer me on.

Before we knew it, it was Thanksgiving, and we traveled to Atlanta to spend it with my Dad. It was our first Thanksgiving without my mom. Everyone wasn't able to travel to Atlanta, but we made the best of the weekend and my twin sister, a niece, Tyrell, Tiffany, and my grandson honored Mom and reminisced. Tiffany had the opportunity to spend some time with her dad who lived twenty minutes from my dad's house. The next day we visited the Georgia Aquarium and ended the day with dinner. We took a lot of pictures and laughed until our faces hurt. My sister, niece, and I headed back home on Saturday, but Tyrell and Tiffany stayed another night. They arrived home late Sunday night. We called it a night, after preparing for work the next day. I left the house before Tyrell and Tiffany. A few hours after arriving at work, I received a call from Tyrell asking if I had the keys to their car. After checking, I said no, and I could tell he was getting irritated because he'd be late for work if he didn't find them soon. I reiterated that I did not have them and to keep searching, they are bound to show up. Well, they did not find the keys, and both ended up calling off work that day. Later Tyrell called me to let me know the neighbor came over and said Tyrell stopped by the night before and left the keys on the table in their garage. Before hanging up, Tyrell said he, Tiffany, and my grandson would spend some quality family time together, go by his aunt's house, and hang out with my older niece and her boyfriend.

While at his aunt's house, they cooked fish, oysters, and shrimp and hung out. While they were cooking, my niece's boyfriend asked Tyrell to drive him to pick up some weed they'd enjoy while cooking. Tyrell agreed since it would only take a few minutes to go there, and he'd come straight back to finish cooking. We don't know what transpired when they got there, but hours later when Tyrell nor my niece's boyfriend had returned, and they got concerned. They tried calling, and finally went to the neighborhood, Tyrell and my niece's boyfriend were headed to. My sister lived near the neighborhood and heard someone had gotten shot. After calling Tyrell several times and getting no answer, they became even more worried. My sisters kept calling me, and I kept calling Tyrell's phone, but he didn't answer. My niece called and told me she heard Tyrell and her boyfriend were shot and the cops had the car taped off. We were certain something happened but not sure exactly what nor did we know whether Tyrell was okay or not. Hours later, we gathered at my house and tried, unsuccessfully, I might add, to reach Tyrell. Sometime later, a detective and the coroner showed up at my house informing me there was a shooting and unfortunately, Tyrell did not survive. I could feel my heart breaking, and I screamed… *"Not my child! You must be mistaken! Where is he!"* 'This cannot be happening,' I thought to myself. 'This must be a dream.'

Later, as the house filled with people, I began to feel claustrophobic. I needed to find solitude. I went into my walk-in closet where it was quiet and dark. I kept telling myself if I stayed in this closet, I would not have to face the reality that Tyrell was murdered by gun violence and never coming back.

My life changed forever on the evening of November 30, 2015. Tyrell was my only child, and he was twenty-three years old. He left behind a wife (his high school sweetheart), Tiffany, and their two-year old son, who was to turn three-years-old only four days later. Tyrell made plans, but they were left undone as we began to plan his funeral. How do you go from planning a three-year old's birthday party to planning his father's funeral? I was having a tough time wrapping my head around having to plan my twenty-three year old son's funeral while attempting to celebrate my three-year old grandson's birthday. A three-year old who was constantly asking for his Daddy because he's unable to understand he'll never see him again. The support, from family and friends, was so immense we had put a note on my front door that we're not receiving visitors that afternoon to celebrate my grandson's birthday. His grandfather came up from North Carolina and had everyone meet at Monkey Joe's. For a moment in time, we were able to escape our reality but only for a few hours. Our hearts were heavy, Tyrell should be here celebrating with his son! This is only one of many Tyrell will never celebrate with his son.

My uncle did an outstanding job officiating and giving the eulogy during Tyrell's funeral. Although it was an emotional day, I remembered him proclaiming that out of Tyrell's death something good would be birthed. As I recall the memory, I remember being irritated with him when he said that and wondered how could good ever come out of this. My child was dead! What good could ever come from this? My heart couldn't comprehend what he was saying, but, over time, I understood it was not for me to understand! Only for me to accept!

I wrestled with my faith after Tyrell and my mother's deaths. The two most important people in my life were gone, without warning. I was angry with God and many people around me just kept telling me *"God does not make mistakes."* They would also tell me *"God will never give me more than I could bare."* My sisters, Nakia and Tanisha, were like second mothers to Tyrell, and they were having a hard time coping as well. We were grieving two deaths during this time, and I found myself not wanting to cry on their shoulders. If they were having a good day, my coming to them with my pain might bring them down. So, I did what so many people do, I suffered in silence! Most days I would isolate myself and think, 'I know people care, but I did not want to bother them.' Clayton was my rock. He was there for me every step and supported me in any and every way possible. I knew he was hurting too and did not want me to witness it. My Aunt Wanda, who was more like a sister to me since we were only a year apart in age, was my go-to and who guided me spiritually. I don't believe she knew how much she helped me get through that period in my life and deal with my anger towards God.

Although an arrest was made no reason was given as to why this young man killed Tyrell and my niece's boyfriend. It was about two and a half years before we went to court. Between my family and the other young man's family members, we packed the courtroom out. Tiffany (Tyrell's wife), his dad, both grandfathers, aunts, great aunts, mother-in-law, Tyrell's cousins, Clayton and I, and the other young man's family and friends were in attendance. We wanted the jury to see the families that these two young men represented. The trial took four days. We listened to testimony from the corner who vividly described Tyrell's and his friend's bodies, their gunshot wounds, and as he identified which bullet(s) caused their death. Not one time did the defendant speak to say why he killed my son and his friend. Ultimately a jury found him guilty, and he was sentenced to two life sentences without the possibility of parole. Even though the verdict brought justice for Tyrell and my niece's boyfriend, it reiterated the fact that when we awoke the next day both young men were still gone! We'd never see them again nor know why their lives were taken.

After many years, I finally chose to be a voice for Tyrell and the many others who have lost their lives to gun violence. I sit on the advisory board of an organization that I co-founded, "Taking Back Our Village." I also co-founded, "We Are Their Voices," a non-profit organization that brings awareness to the effects of gun violence and offers support to families and communities. I joined my local "Moms Demand Chapter" volunteering as the Community Outreach Lead, and I serve as the South Carolina Deputy Chapter Lead and an Everytown for Gun Safety Survivor Fellow.

As Tyrell's Mom and spokesperson, I am that voice that honors his memory and shares memories of him with his son. A few years ago, I met with a spiritual advisor who gave me insight into Tyrell's death and told me all my suffering was over. Although I might not understand, everything that occurred had to happen for me to fulfill my purpose in life. This took me back to what my uncle and Pastor said at Tyrell's funeral, "...*something good would come out of Tyrell's death.*" I have awoken many mornings and thought about the many times I was referred to Psalm 30:5, "*Weeping may endure for the night, but joy cometh in the morning.*" I know that God does not operate on a twenty-four-hour clock nor a yearly calendar, but I know my morning is coming. I have the power to create the change I want to see and by sharing my faith in God during the darkest and the hardest moments in my life, I can help others through the things they don't believe they can survive.

In Loving Memory:
Tyrell Miles

JOURNAL PROMPT

As I was thinking of what my chapter title should be named, I thought of the many unforeseen milestones over his twenty-three years and where it brought us to now. What traumatic milestones have you endured in life and how have you been able to overcome them?

_____

_____

_____

_____

_____

_____

_____

_____

_____

_____

_____

_____

_____

_____

_____

_____

Photo Credit – Upscale Images

CHAPTER 10: Author - Julvonnia McDowell

Julvonnia Young-McDowell grew up in the hostess city of Savannah, GA. She is a strong woman of Faith, a proud Army wife and Navy mom. Julvonnia holds a B.A in Psychology and will soon be working towards her Master of Arts Degree. She is the 2020 Remarkable Woman recipient representing her hometown of Savannah, GA. She is on the path to making a difference in the world due to the unnatural title of gun violence survivor. She discovered journaling and writing poetry to be therapeutic after her 14-year-old son's life was taken tragically in 2016 by an unintentional shooting incident.

Julvonnia was determined not to allow her grief to define her but to elevate her to be a motivator for others. She believes that in spite of the grief, you can overcome, and you can PRESS: Persevere, Rise,

Emerge, Smile and Shine. Julvonnia started advocating about the importance and urgency of gun safety. She is a mentor to youth by teaching them not to allow their environment to dictate their path. She is a co-host to an upcoming Podcast of women living beyond grief and she is working on her second book.

Not only is she an advocate for gun safety and prevention, she also is an activist on issues of oppression, racial disparities, and gender equity. Julvonnia is a woman determined to save lives by sharing her story of rising and living beyond a tragedy. She has shared her survivor story with an array of audiences and has graced the stage with many powerful men and women to include President Joe Biden, and Senator Bernie Sanders. She has also had the opportunity to share the stage with Dr. Jill Biden with the launch of Moms for Biden campaign. Julvonnia is a part of the National Anthem for the Be SMART campaign to foster a community of responsible gun ownership, gun safety, and taking actions to ensure the safety and well-being of our children *https://besmartforkids.org/*.

Julvonnia stated that she was no longer going to sit on the sidelines, but she was determined to get in the game. She has also had the honor to speak with and share a discussion with Senator Elizabeth Warren during Demanding Women: Quarantine Conversations about gun violence. She was featured with Congresswoman Lucy McBath in Vogue magazine, and many other Congressional leaders to talk about the importance of ending gun violence. She has also spoken at the Pediatric Associates Societies and at Emory University "SAFE" and "Ask" campaigns. Her stories have been featured in Essence, Vogue, Humanity, and People Magazines. Her favorite quote is that by Dr. Martin Luther King, Jr. *"Darkness cannot drive out darkness; only light can do that. Hate cannot drive out hate; only love can do that."*

CHAPTER 10: EMERGING STRENGTH

By

Julvonnia McDowell

"Experiences in life have a way of knocking one down, but it is not until you decree that you will no longer stay there. You emerge strengthened from within to rise and stand again."
-Julvonnia McDowell

JaJuan was getting ready and prepared to enter his first year of high school. August could not come fast enough for an eighth-grader, eagerly looking forward to his high school years. He often talked about the excitement of becoming a freshman, how he was going to walk the halls and that the entire school was going to know his name from his grades and athletic abilities. We would laugh and respond, *"Bud, yes, they will."* We noticed his confidence growing day by day. JaJuan stated that he was going to be like his big brother TJ and be crowned best dressed for his junior-senior prom. The excitement could be heard in his voice when he spoke about prom, graduation, and entering college. He often referenced these milestones before adulthood.

High school was waiting, but we, as parents often thought, this is *getting too real.* My husband and I often joked about becoming empty nesters. Wow, four more years, and we will have a senior in college and a senior in high school. Our sons were four years apart in age and grade levels. As parents, we imagined both walking across the stage as honor graduates.

A conversation that we had often was how college life would be for them and the joy of decorating their dorms. We laughed about who would shed tears first as we dropped them off. I imagined the daily calls. I knew that I would be a pest because I talked to my children daily. They would say, *"Mommy, we are growing up."* I would often get emotional thinking about it. A smile would often emerge, knowing that I would still hear their voices daily. Little did they know I needed them just as much as they needed me. They gave me the necessary strength to keep going. Watching our sons become adults, get married, and have children of their own; is what we as parents anticipate in our golden years.

On Monday, March 7th, 2016, our day was filled with laughter, joy, and love. We surprised our son, JaJuan, after school, with his favorite Chocolate Chip Bundt cake. The way his eyes lit up from the surprise just melted our hearts. He blew out his candles to commemorate his 14th birthday. We reminisced about past birthdays and who received the best gifts. We talked about life, health, wealth, and the future, not realizing the significance of this conversation. JaJuan talked about life without being physically present, and we would correct him, but he continued to talk that way. He would say, "I am not going to be here forever." I would come back and say, "Bud, you are not going anywhere, but to bed." Later that night, I asked my husband did that conversation sound normal. He responded, "Babe, *you know how JaJuan is,"* but it was something different.

As a mother, I prayed a daily prayer that my sons would become the men God created, destined, and purposed for them to be, live abundantly, and nurture a relationship with Him. The inconceivable occurred just one month later. As you can imagine, I never saw it coming!

On Thursday, April 7th, 2016, I was downstairs getting ready to start dinner. My husband had just gotten home from work and was heading upstairs to take a shower. As I was preparing his favorite meal, my cell phone began ringing. I checked to see who was calling and it said TJ, my blessing. My first response was to finish dinner, then return TJ's call, but I had an overwhelming feeling that I needed to answer the call. I answered with excitement, *"Hey son, how is it going? What are you and JaJuan doing?"* There was a long pause. TJ asked, *"Where is dad? Are you sitting down?"* I responded *"Why? What is going on?"* The next words left me cradled on the floor screaming. TJ said, *"Mommy, it does not look good. JaJuan has been shot. Hurry! Hurry!"* I could not think of what to ask. The only words I could say in a complete sentence were, *"Lord, let my child be okay."* My husband heard my screams. I got up enough strength to say, *"Our baby's been shot."* My husband began to weep, and we held each other while trying to muster up enough calmness to drive four hours to the unknown.

My body went numb; pain pierced every fiber of my existence, and my heart broke into a million pieces. I had so many questions. I could not think of what to ask or even how to ask if he was okay. I just needed him to be alive. As we left the house, I could not remember if we cut off the lights, the stove, set the alarm, or locked the doors. We were so frantic that we could not remember the way to the highway. I was unable to process anything. I was experiencing an overwhelming pain pressing against my spine. I was sinking, drowning in the pain of my tears, to the point that no one could resuscitate me. I began to try to make calls to family members and friends to inform them of JaJuan's condition. We called our Pastor, and he could hear the pain and urgency in my voice, *"JaJuan has been shot."* He prayed with us and said he would meet us at the hospital.

We arrived at the hospital in time to hear, *"he did not make it."* JaJuan succumbed to his injuries seventeen minutes after I answered that dreadful call. Everything about strength and hope was so far from my mind, but I knew I needed God, my family, and friends. I could not think straight. My heart was racing with every beat. Each time my heart fought to slow down, my thoughts caused my heart to beat faster and louder. My husband was trying to console me while tears poured from his eyes. As he gazed into my eyes and I gazed into his eyes, pain stared back. I never guessed or imagined for a moment when our sons strode out the door, that it would be the last time we would see them together. We went from a family of four and in an instant to a family of three. I kept recalling the last time. Four hours before that call, I called JaJuan. During the conversation, he had plans to go to the movies with his grandmother at six that evening. I said, *"Bud, tell me all about the movie when you get back. Be safe, and I love you, Bud."* He responded, *"Okay, Mommy, I love you too".* That is the last *'I love you'* I will ever hear from him.

After leaving the hospital, we arrived at my mother's home. We were greeted, comforted, and surrounded by family, church family, and friends. All of whom we needed and still need even now. They are an intricate part of our healing. Upon speaking with the detective, I learned JaJuan was unintentionally shot and killed by a thirteen-year-old playing with an unsecured firearm; everything about this investigation imploded in agony. The pain etched into every fiber of my being, and it flowed deep beneath my veins. I was experiencing a grief journey that took away my identity, resulting in me struggling emotionally. To look at me, no one would imagine I was fighting to be present now.

The investigation into JaJuan's death took more out of me than I wanted or was willing to give. However, no matter how much my strength wavered while on this journey, it can never compare to who was taken from me. I learned grief had many faces, and the one I was experiencing at that moment was that of betrayal. The detective called and stated they were charging the thirteen-year-old with involuntary manslaughter. Now, I am facing a situation that I cannot comprehend. Do I advocate for judicial justice for my child, or do I attempt to assist the child that unintentionally killed my baby? The more I think about it, the more I realize I do not want to comprehend it; I need peace. Accidental shooting is what someone labeled the incident, but it was 100 percent preventable. My mind cannot process the distinction between unintentional and intentional because my child should still be alive.

We witnessed someone who was considered family entering a path that I wish on no one. Eleven months earlier, we opened our arms and doors for this child. Here we are again, two close families grieving from an unhealed opened wound.

This child witnessed his fifteen-year-old brother get shot and killed in front of him. Lord, this is too much. I asked the detective about his thoughts on speaking with him. I also inquired what options did we have because this was too close for comfort. He stated that the medical examiner ruled JaJuan's death a homicide; and that I could speak with the child to ascertain if he would tell the truth. He had already given several misleading statements and stories that never matched the physical evidence. I figured *he loved JaJuan enough to tell me the truth.*

In September 2016, we were sitting in the courtroom; amongst the pain that sat with me was a feeling of empathy. What I saw was a scared little boy lacking emotions and unable to comprehend what was happening. The trial lasted one day, and he pled guilty to involuntary manslaughter. So many emotions because hurt, grief, and pain divided two close families. I experienced an awakening and quickening in my spirit. I sat on that hard bench, experiencing emotion after emotion. I was trying to process the Judge's sentencing order, and somehow finding solace amid the pain. I could hear God saying, *"I am with you. Remember to breathe."*

During this grief journey, I began to search for the unknown and get in tune with my spiritual being. I began to look at each mark on my canvas. So much emerged from the hurt, the trial, the agony, the betrayal, and the isolation that I never knew existed. The day came, and I was ready to address the grief. There were so many dynamics and components of grief. It required me to learn how to live all over again. I had to learn how to speak again. Speaking to the hurt was not an easy task. I had to be vulnerable to my feelings. The uneasiness was so intense that I needed to address it. I needed to engage my heart, my mind, my soul, and my emotions. It was a new Julvonnia, a healing mother, that had the power within but could not find her until I was ready to hold the paintbrush again. It was challenging to learn how to navigate my life and at the same time accept pain as my constant companion. In the same way, it is a painful reality not having my son physically present with me every day.

Until I was ready to face my grief, I read 1 Peter 4:12 (ESV), *"Beloved, do not be surprised at the fiery trial when it comes upon you to test you, as though something strange was happening to you."* There was a time when I questioned my existence, and I felt like a stranger in my heart and mind. There was a period I often thought that I had failed as a mother because I was not there to protect and save my son. The title of gun violence survivor was a struggle to accept; it was a challenge to comprehend the meaning of this unnatural title. I struggled to enjoy life. I needed to dig deep to restore my sense of being. I examined every fiber of my being as I gazed in the mirror. I began to speak to her as she stared at me. I noticed the uncertainty and yearning to be found again in her eyes. A piece of me was seeking a peace that had been lost for so long. My emotions were on a roller coaster and were emerging from an impossibly low place.

Philippians 4:13, "*I can do all things through Christ, who strengthens me.*" I had some redefining moments that emerged from time to time. They left me feeling weak, with no strength to speak of, without God's love, power, forgiveness, protection, peace, and guidance. Then I remembered Philippians 4:13 and admitted to myself; I do not know where I would be without His steady presence in my life. It has helped me emerge from the pain, guilt, shame, and hurt. I stand in my authority and declare my healing and peace. Yes, I have been through the fire. I know that if it had not been for the Lord, who was not only on my side but within me, I would not be here today. I emerged to declare it was not my strength but God's strength. It is made perfect in the weakness I drew from daily. There was a time I could not say my son was no longer here physically, but today I can say it and can feel his presence.

It was not until I was ready to face, speak to, and grab the paintbrush to grow out of those dark places I concealed for so long. I found the courage to allow myself to discover my strength in my willingness to be vulnerable. My strength was not in how much I could carry on my shoulders during this season. My strength was not in how much I could pack in my heart, no matter how heavy the day was when it unfolded. My strength was not in the stretch when being pulled in different directions. My strength was not in my tolerance of how much I could take or in surviving tragedies. My strength was buried in a place waiting to emerge and bloom like a flower full of grace. My gift to myself was to keep growing, pressing, pushing, and living despite this enduring grief.

Here is a poem that I wrote on this healing journey in memory of a sweet little boy that entered my heart, grew in my womb, and filled us with love. I titled it "Time" So often, time is something we hope for, but the realization is time is something we cannot get back or replace. Time is beautifully wrapped in a cocoon awaiting its assignment and season to emerge with strength and time to soar like a Butterfly.

TIME

by Julvonnia McDowell

We remember sitting and thinking this cannot be it. We thought we
had more time to finish.

We had so much on our to-do list.

Like seeing all those birthday wishes, hopes and dreams come into
existence.

Fourteen candles you blew out on March 7th, 2016, and made
birthday wishes.

Wishes we will never know, get to ask about, or see fulfilled.

Be Still.

But we knew there was time to complete.

Complete all your dreams.

Accomplish and achieve all your goals: which included walking across
the stage a proud graduate of the class of 2020.

Some may reference it as a time of bleakness.

We still had places to visit, schools to attend, things to see, people to
meet, and dreams to speak.

We still had College tours to seek.

But what happens when things are left incomplete.

What happens when you can no longer complete your checklist or
fulfill those activities that are now missing?

It leaves a void that seems hard to fill.

Be Still.

It may seem easy to do, but what happens when the pain sticks like
glue?

We do not get a chance to speak those words that are now left
unspoken.

We did not get a chance to complete those tasks that we never
imagined as our last.

We wonder if we could even handle getting that chance to say see you later at that moment.

Our minds seem to think so, but our hearts are fluttering with so many emotions.

Be Still.

In Loving Memory:
JaJuan Ziontae McDowell

JOURNAL PROMPT

In life there are situations, circumstances, and experiences that have a way of changing us, transforming us, and giving us insight through a different lens. What has transpired in your life that has prompted you to change your period to a comma? What are ways in which you plan to keep going despite the pain?

_____

_____

_____

_____

_____

_____

_____

_____

_____

_____

_____

_____

_____

_____

AUTHOR CONTACT INFORMATION

Author	Email Address
DeAndra Dycus	hello@deandradycus.com www.deandradycus.com www.purpose4mypain.org
Julvonnia McDowell	julvonniamcdowell@gmail.com www.julvonniamcdowell.org
Valeria Horton	jayvaslove@outlook.com
Falisha Curlin Walker	Falishacurlin@gmail.com
Thomasena Colbert	tommicolbert76@gmail.com
Wendy McIntosh	wendymcintosh@ymail.com
Tisa Whack	tisawhack@gmail.com www.wearetheirvoices.com
Stephanie Stone	stephlstone68@gmail.com
Olga Williams	olgalotowilliams@gmail.com www.dominquesworld.org/
Pamela Wooden	8530walt@gmail

Denola M. Burton
DenolaBurton@EnhancedDNA1.com
www.EnhancedDNAPublishing.com

Made in the USA
Coppell, TX
23 December 2021

69969271R00090